DIVINE MOMENTS FOR MEN

Everyday Inspiration from God's Word

DIVINE MOMENTS

MOMENTS

for

MEN

Everyday Inspiration

from God's Word

Tyndale House Publishers, Inc.

Carol Stream, Illinois

Visit Tyndale's exciting Web site at www.tyndale.com

Divine Moments for Men: Everyday Inspiration from God's Word

Managing editors: Ronald A. Beers and Amy E. Mason

Contributing writers: V. Gilbert Beers, Rebecca J. Beers, Brian R. Coffey, Jonathan Farrar, Jeffrey Frasier, Jonathan Gray, Shawn A. Harrison, Sandy Hull, Rhonda K. O'Brien, Douglas J. Rumford, Linda Taylor

Designed by Julie Chen

Edited by Michal Needham

ISBN-13: 978-1-4143-1227-9

ISBN-10: 1-4143-1227-X

Printed in the United States of America

14 13 12 11 10 09 08

7 6 5 4 3 2 1

Introduction

The goal of *Divine Moments for Men* is to help you experience a breakthrough with God, to show you how and where God is at work in your life to get your attention each day. If the Bible is really a blueprint for living, then God, through his Word, should be able to respond to any question you have for him. And he does! As you read the questions and Scripture in this book, it is amazing to see how God's answers to your daily needs are so clear and help you see with "spiritual eyes" how he is trying to break through to you. Sometimes God seems so big and mysterious that you may wonder whether he would truly bother with you. But he loves you personally and is trying to get your attention every day. This little book can help you notice the divine moments when he is trying to show you how much he cares. You can read straight through the book, or you can use it topically when you are looking for God's help in a certain area of life or if you just need more clarity about what God might say about something important to you. We pray this little book will be meaningful to you and help you experience many divine moments with God.

—The editors

Abilities

How do I maximize my God-given abilities?

A MOMENT *with* GOD

Samson judged Israel for twenty years during the
period when the Philistines dominated the land. . . .
One day Samson went to the Philistine town of Gaza
and spent the night with a prostitute. . . . Delilah
lulled Samson to sleep with his head in her lap,
and then she called in a man to shave off the seven
locks of his hair. In this way she began to bring him
down, and his strength left him. Then she cried out,
"Samson! The Philistines have come to capture you!"
When he woke up, he thought, "I will do as before
and shake myself free." But he didn't realize the LORD
had left him.   JUDGES 15:20; 16:1, 19-20

With a man like Samson, Israel should have been rul-
ing the Philistines, not the other way around. How
ironic that a woman—certainly smaller than Samson—brought him down! The strongest do not always
prevail, the fastest do not always win, the smartest do
not always finish at the top of their class. God-given
abilities are only maximized when they are used for
God-given purposes. A dollar bill is useless if a vend-
ing machine takes only coins. Samson's great strength
became useless when he used it to do something that
didn't fit God's plan. Do you know what your God-
given abilities are? These are sometimes called spiritual

gifts. One of the first breakthroughs in the Christian life is discovering the abilities God has given you. Then when you learn how to use those gifts for him, not just for yourself, you will experience a profound divine moment. Fit your God-given abilities into God's plan, and watch your life produce great results.

DIVINE PROMISE

WHEN SOMEONE HAS BEEN GIVEN MUCH, MUCH WILL BE REQUIRED IN RETURN; AND WHEN SOMEONE HAS BEEN ENTRUSTED WITH MUCH, EVEN MORE WILL BE REQUIRED. *Luke 12:48*

Accomplishments

MY QUESTION *for* GOD

I'm just an ordinary person; there's nothing special about me. Can God accomplish anything through me?

A MOMENT *with* GOD

The members of the council were amazed when they saw the boldness of Peter and John, for they could see that they were ordinary men with no special training in the Scriptures. They also recognized them as men who had been with Jesus. ACTS 4:13

Live in harmony with each other. Don't be too proud to enjoy the company of ordinary people. ROMANS 12:16

This message was given to Amos, a shepherd from the town of Tekoa in Judah. AMOS 1:1

Samuel asked, "Are these all the sons you have?" "There is still the youngest," Jesse replied. "But he's out in the fields watching the sheep and goats." . . . The LORD said, "This is the one; anoint him."

1 SAMUEL 16:11-12

Although God sometimes uses miracles and angels to accomplish his plans, he more often chooses ordinary people doing ordinary things to accomplish something extraordinary. One day God may call you to do something extraordinary, but meanwhile get to work serving and obeying him today. Then you'll be ready when he calls.

DIVINE PROMISE

GOD CHOSE THINGS THE WORLD CONSIDERS FOOLISH IN ORDER TO SHAME THOSE WHO THINK THEY ARE WISE. AND HE CHOSE THINGS THAT ARE POWERLESS TO SHAME THOSE WHO ARE POWERFUL. *1 Corinthians 1:27*

Accomplishments

MY QUESTION *for* GOD

How do I accomplish things that will last?

A MOMENT *with* GOD

They began saying to each other, "Let's make bricks
and harden them with fire." . . . Then they said,
"Come, let's build a great city for ourselves with a
tower that reaches into the sky. This will make us
famous and keep us from being scattered all over the
world." But the LORD came down to look at the city
and the tower the people were building. "Look!" he
said. "The people are united, and they all speak the
same language. After this, nothing they set out to do
will be impossible for them! Come, let's go down and
confuse the people with different languages. Then
they won't be able to understand each other." In that
way, the LORD scattered them all over the world, and
they stopped building the city.   GENESIS 11:3-8

*D*eep within the human heart lies a God-given long-
ing for significance and lasting accomplishment. But
too often we have much lower ambitions. It's easy to
look out for ourselves. It's more difficult, more costly,
more significant to look out for others. If our ambition
is merely to look out for ourselves, we waste the opportunity for our accomplishments to last into eternity.
Sadly, we become like ants who build their hill on a
sidewalk and proudly proclaim, "Look! It will stand
forever." We must always be asking ourselves if our passion and purpose is to accomplish things that (a) glorify
ourselves, which are only temporary and do not last
beyond this life, or (b) glorify God by serving others,
which are lasting and bring eternal rewards.

DIVINE PROMISE

THEY SHOULD BE RICH IN GOOD WORKS
AND GENEROUS TO THOSE IN NEED, ALWAYS
BEING READY TO SHARE WITH OTHERS. BY
DOING THIS THEY WILL BE STORING UP THEIR
TREASURE AS A GOOD FOUNDATION FOR
THE FUTURE SO THAT THEY MAY EXPERIENCE
TRUE LIFE. *1 Timothy 6:18-19*

Accountability

MY QUESTION *for* GOD

How can accountability deepen my relationship with God?

A MOMENT *with* GOD

"Can anyone hide from me in a secret place? Am I
not everywhere in all the heavens and earth?" says
the LORD. JEREMIAH 23:24

You must commit yourselves wholeheartedly to these
commands that I am giving you today. Repeat them
again and again to your children. Talk about them
when you are at home and when you are on the road,
when you are going to bed and when you are getting
up. Tie them to your hands and wear them on your
forehead as reminders. Write them on the doorposts
of your house and on your gates. . . . Do what is
right and good in the LORD's sight, so all will go well
with you. DEUTERONOMY 6:6-9, 18

To be accountable means you have to answer to someone. To be unaccountable means you freely go wherever your desires lead. Accountability is literally giving an account of yourself—where you've been, what you've been doing, what your motives were. The one who is holding you accountable has the freedom to ask for this account from you. The purpose of accountability is not to keep you from having fun but to help you enjoy life even more by preventing you from impulsively doing something that will hurt yourself or someone else. With the right person holding you accountable, you will make better decisions that will positively impact your future. You may not always like to be held accountable; you may think it puts too many restrictions on you. It forces you to open up the dark corners of your life that you'd prefer to keep hidden. But accountability will keep you honest, happy, and on the right path. It's not always comfortable, but it's necessary. Ultimately, accountability means answering to God. If you're really going to take it seriously, you have to begin with God as your primary accountability partner. He knows all the secrets of your heart anyway, so why try to hide anything from him? Be honest with God, and tell him about your struggles. Follow his principles for living as found in the Bible. Then you'll be less likely to do something you will later regret. You will better understand what you are doing and why you are doing it when you understand for whom you are doing it.

DIVINE PROMISE

YOU WILL ALWAYS HARVEST WHAT YOU PLANT.

Galatians 6:7

Addiction

MY QUESTION *for* GOD

How can God break the power of addiction in my life?

A MOMENT *with* GOD

You say, "I am allowed to do anything"—but not everything is good for you. And even though "I am allowed to do anything," I must not become a slave to anything. 1 CORINTHIANS 6:12

Don't copy the behavior and customs of this world, but let God transform you into a new person by changing the way you think. Then you will learn to know God's will for you, which is good and pleasing and perfect. ROMANS 12:2

You belong to God, my dear children. You have already won a victory over those people, because the Spirit who lives in you is greater than the spirit who lives in the world. 1 JOHN 4:4

The Holy Spirit produces this kind of fruit in our lives: love, joy, peace, patience, kindness, goodness, faithfulness, gentleness, and self-control.

GALATIANS 5:22-23

Who in their right mind would volunteer to become a slave, chained forever to a life of bondage? That's exactly what addiction is: self-imposed slavery. It's selling yourself into a lifetime of bondage to a habit or substance. While we often think of addiction as a problem related to drugs or alcohol, there are other addictions that are just as destructive. You can become addicted to laziness, watching television, playing computer games, eating unhealthy food—the list goes on and on. You can even become addicted to good things, like exercising too much or eating too much health food. We all have our addictions, whether they are simply bad habits or serious dependencies. Sin is the worst addiction. Like other addictive habits or substances, sin often appears alluring and attractive and promises short-term pleasure. You can easily justify giving in just this once, thinking you have things under control. But soon you realize that your "one time" has turned into a habit you can't stop. It now controls you. As with other addictions, sin often results when you lose your self-control. Ironically, the only way to recover self-control is to let God control you. His control is always for your benefit and for your spiritual growth. God can break the power of any addiction you are struggling with when you give him control of your life. It is imperative that you admit your addiction and acknowledge its destructiveness. God often works through other people to help you. It is almost impossible to overcome addiction by yourself; you need the consistent support of people who love you enough to tell you the truth and hold you accountable. But you must also hold yourself accountable to God's way of living, as written in the Bible. This will keep you close to God, and he will work in your life to change your heart and desires. Surrender to the Holy Spirit, and God will replace addictive impulses with life-affirming desires. While it is important to seek the

$\mathcal{N}$o one is wise enough to anticipate all the complexities of a situation or grasp all the issues related to a problem. Good advisers bring perspective, information, expertise, and experience to whatever challenges and problems you face. The right counsel can make the difference between success and failure, joy and sorrow, prosperity and poverty, victory and defeat.

Divine Promise

YOU GUIDE ME WITH YOUR COUNSEL, LEADING ME TO A GLORIOUS DESTINY. *Psalm 73:24*

Affirmation

My Questions *for* God

The daily grind can be pretty tough. Does God really care? Is he on my side?

A Moment *with* God

Surely your goodness and unfailing love will pursue me all the days of my life. *Psalm 23:6*

I will be glad and rejoice in your unfailing love, for you have seen my troubles, and you care about the anguish of my soul. *Psalm 31:7*

No eye has seen, no ear has heard, and no mind has imagined what God has prepared for those who love him. *1 Corinthians 2:9*

The LORD is like a father to his children, tender and compassionate to those who fear him.   PSALM 103:13

We all have a need to be affirmed. We want to know that our life has value and is valued by others. Unfortunately, people don't always offer the affirmation we need, and as a result we might feel rejected, alone, or worthless. When no one else gives you words of affirmation, you can still feel affirmed because the almighty God chose to create you in his image and longs to be in relationship with you. He sent his own Son to die for your sins so that you could have the opportunity to live with him forever. God's words and actions toward you affirm that he desires your heart and soul, and that you matter to him. When you realize just how passionate God is about you, you can experience a breakthrough in your spiritual life. You will begin to notice all the little ways he interrupts your day with a blessing here and an encouragement there. The more you see with spiritual eyes the daily evidence of God's love for you, the more confident and affirmed you will feel.

DIVINE PROMISE

MAY GOD BE MERCIFUL AND BLESS US. MAY HIS FACE SMILE WITH FAVOR ON US.   *Psalm 67:1*

Agreement

MY QUESTION *for* GOD

How can I live in today's culture without compromising my convictions?

A MOMENT *with* GOD

Daniel was determined not to defile himself by eating the food and wine given to them by the king. He asked the chief of staff for permission not to eat these unacceptable foods. . . . "Please test us for ten days on a diet of vegetables and water," Daniel said. . . . The attendant agreed to Daniel's suggestion. . . . At the end of the ten days, Daniel and his three friends looked healthier and better nourished than the young men who had been eating the food assigned by the king.

DANIEL 1:8, 12, 14-15

When trying to reach an agreement, there is a time to compromise and a time to hold firm. When the forces of evil tempt you to give up your convictions, you cannot budge. To compromise God's truth, God's ways, or God's Word is to negotiate with that which is unholy. The test of acceptable compromise is simple: Can you reach an agreement that satisfies both parties without sacrificing anyone's morals? If you give up godliness in exchange for anything else, it's a bad bargain. Work for harmony and agreement whenever possible, but when it is not possible, pray that God would break through the stalemate to make his will clear.

DIVINE CHALLENGE

PUT ON ALL OF GOD'S ARMOR SO THAT YOU
WILL BE ABLE TO STAND FIRM AGAINST ALL
STRATEGIES OF THE DEVIL.   *Ephesians 6:11*

Ambition

MY QUESTION *for* GOD

Can ambition be good?

A MOMENT *with* GOD

Joyful are people of integrity, who follow the
instructions of the LORD. Joyful are those who . . .
search for him with all their hearts.   PSALM 119:1-2

Make it your goal to live a quiet life, minding your
own business and working with your hands, just as
we instructed you before.   1 THESSALONIANS 4:11

My ambition has always been to preach the Good
News where the name of Christ has never been heard.

ROMANS 15:20

*A*mbition can be compared to fire—both have the
potential to be powerfully productive or terribly destructive. When fire is kept in a fireplace, it produces
heat and light. But when it is used improperly, fire
threatens to consume everything in its path. So it is
with ambition. The Bible encourages us to learn to distinguish between godly ambition, which can produce

great benefits, and selfish ambition, which can blaze
out of control. Godly ambition yields a burning desire
to know God and do what he asks. Selfish ambition
produces the desire to bring credit and glory to yourself rather than to God. You can test your ambition by
asking yourself this question: Is it leading you closer to
God or farther away from him? If you're not sure, then
most likely it is leading you away from him.

DIVINE CHALLENGE

JESUS SAID TO HIS DISCIPLES, "IF ANY OF YOU
WANTS TO BE MY FOLLOWER, YOU MUST TURN
FROM YOUR SELFISH WAYS, TAKE UP YOUR
CROSS, AND FOLLOW ME." *Matthew 16:24*

Anger

MY QUESTION *for* GOD

Why do I get angry?

A MOMENT *with* GOD

The LORD accepted Abel and his gift, but he did not
accept Cain and his gift. This made Cain very angry,
and he looked dejected.   GENESIS 4:4-5

"You have made me look like a fool!" Balaam shouted.
NUMBERS 22:29

"Didn't I tell you?" the king of Israel exclaimed to
Jehoshaphat. "He never prophesies anything but

trouble for me. . . . Put this man in prison, and feed
him nothing but bread and water!"   1 KINGS 22:18, 27

"Get out of the sanctuary, for you have sinned."
. . . Uzziah, who was holding an incense burner,
became furious.   2 CHRONICLES 26:18-19

When Haman saw that Mordecai would not bow
down or show him respect, he was filled with rage.

                                       ESTHER 3:5

*A*nger is often a reaction to your pride being hurt.
When you are confronted, rejected, ignored, or don't
get your way, anger acts as a defense mechanism to
protect your ego. It is common to feel angry when
someone confronts you about your own sinful actions
because you don't want others to know that you've
done something wrong. When anger begins to well up
inside you, stop and ask yourself, *Who is really offended
in this situation? Is this about God's honor or my pride? Am I
acting out of humility or revenge?* Confession, forgiveness,
and reconciliation will melt your anger away.

DIVINE PROMISE

A GENTLE ANSWER DEFLECTS ANGER, BUT
HARSH WORDS MAKE TEMPERS FLARE.
Proverbs 15:1

Apathy

MY QUESTION *for* GOD

Sometimes I just don't care anymore. Does it matter if I feel this way?

A MOMENT *with* GOD

They have made it an empty wasteland; I hear its mournful cry. The whole land is desolate, and no one even cares.

JEREMIAH 12:11

What makes us think we can escape if we ignore this great salvation that was first announced by the Lord Jesus himself and then delivered to us by those who heard him speak?

HEBREWS 2:3

*I*ronically, apathy can cause you to lose what you most want. If you are apathetic toward your wife, you are in danger of losing her. If you are apathetic about investing your money, you are in danger of losing your retirement income. If you are apathetic toward God, you are in danger of losing the priceless rewards that await his followers in heaven. Apathy often seems to be a passive force that simply lulls you to sleep, but it can also be an aggressive force that prevents you from keeping what is most meaningful and important to you.

Divine Challenge

WATCH OUT THAT YOU DO NOT LOSE WHAT
WE HAVE WORKED SO HARD TO ACHIEVE.
BE DILIGENT SO THAT YOU RECEIVE YOUR
FULL REWARD.   *2 John 1:8*

Apology

My Question *for* God

*Is it really that important to apologize when I've done
something wrong?*

A Moment *with* God

The high and lofty one who lives in eternity, the Holy
One, says this: "I live in the high and holy place with
those whose spirits are contrite and humble. I restore
the crushed spirit of the humble and revive the
courage of those with repentant hearts."   ISAIAH 57:15

Confess your sins to each other and pray for each
other so that you may be healed.   JAMES 5:16

Saying "I'm sorry" for something you have done
wrong is one of the most difficult things to do. You
have to recognize your fault, face it head-on, and then
humble yourself enough to admit it to someone else. A
sincere apology is the first step in changing your behavior and committing to do the right thing. Refusing to
apologize when you know you're wrong is a clear sign
of pride, which can have devastating effects on your

life and relationships. But being willing to apologize
demonstrates humility and opens the door to healing
and blessing. If you need a breakthrough in your relationship with a coworker, a loved one, or God himself,
the practice of admitting when you are wrong will help
you reach a new level of trust and respect.

Divine Promise

PEOPLE WHO CONCEAL THEIR SINS WILL
NOT PROSPER, BUT IF THEY CONFESS AND
TURN FROM THEM, THEY WILL RECEIVE
MERCY. BLESSED ARE THOSE WHO FEAR TO DO
WRONG, BUT THE STUBBORN ARE HEADED FOR
SERIOUS TROUBLE.   *Proverbs 28:13-14*

Apology

My Question *for* God

How do I accept an apology?

A Moment *with* God

So he returned home to his father. And while he
was still a long way off, his father saw him coming.
Filled with love and compassion, he ran to his son,
embraced him, and kissed him. His son said to him,
"Father, I have sinned against both heaven and you,
and I am no longer worthy of being called your son."
But his father said to the servants, "Quick! Bring the
finest robe in the house and put it on him. Get a ring

for his finger and sandals for his feet. And kill the
calf we have been fattening. We must celebrate with
a feast, for this son of mine was dead and has now
returned to life. He was lost, but now he is found."
So the party began.   LUKE 15:20-24

When someone who has wronged you apologizes, you
might be tempted to punish the person further, to lash
out in anger, to make him or her suffer a little more.
But in this parable that Jesus told, not only did the Father forgive his son at once, he also called for a party to
celebrate this great event—his son's being restored to
his family. True forgiveness is not grudging or sparing
but generous, joyful, and healing. When you accept an
apology in this way, you will create a divine moment
in the other person's life by showing the same kind of
mercy God shows when he forgives you.

DIVINE PROMISE

FINALLY, I CONFESSED ALL MY SINS TO YOU
AND STOPPED TRYING TO HIDE MY GUILT.
I SAID TO MYSELF, "I WILL CONFESS MY
REBELLION TO THE LORD." AND YOU FORGAVE
ME! ALL MY GUILT IS GONE.   *Psalm 32:5*

Approval

MY QUESTION *for* GOD

So often I want to be approved by others, but I know God's approval is more important. How do I properly balance these two priorities?

A MOMENT *with* GOD

We speak as messengers approved by God to be entrusted with the Good News. Our purpose is to please God, not people. He alone examines the motives of our hearts.   1 THESSALONIANS 2:4

The Kingdom of God is not a matter of what we eat or drink, but of living a life of goodness and peace and joy in the Holy Spirit. If you serve Christ with this attitude, you will please God, and others will approve of you, too.   ROMANS 14:17-18

What causes us to approve of some people and not others? Too often it comes down to appearance or performance. We don't like the way someone looks, or we don't like something they've done. Or perhaps the shoe is on the other foot, and you find it hard to win the approval of someone you love or someone you work for. You may never earn the approval of certain people, no matter how good you look or how well you perform. When evaluating your desire for approval, you should understand the ground rules. It's entirely appropriate for your boss to disapprove of your work if you are not meeting set standards of performance. It's entirely

appropriate for God to disapprove of your behavior
if you are enjoying a lifestyle that is contrary to his
commandments. But there's another kind of approval
that everyone needs, and it should never be based on
performance. It is the unconditional love we all long
for. In a good family, you find love and acceptance no
matter how you look or what you do. This is a picture
of what it's like to be in God's family. As a child of
God, created in his image, God loves and accepts you
not for what you do but for who you are. The fact that
God has created you gives you great worth. He loves
you and approves of you because you are his, no matter
what you think about him or what others think about
you. The knowledge that nothing you can do will cause
God to love you less should give you peace of mind and
motivate you to please him even more.

DIVINE CHALLENGE

ACCEPT EACH OTHER JUST AS CHRIST HAS
ACCEPTED YOU SO THAT GOD WILL BE
GIVEN GLORY.   *Romans 15:7*

Assurance

MY QUESTION *for* GOD

How can I be sure God is calling me to do something specific?

A MOMENT *with* GOD

After the death of Moses the LORD's servant, the
LORD spoke to Joshua son of Nun, Moses' assistant.
He said, "Moses my servant is dead. Therefore, the
time has come for you to lead these people, the
Israelites, across the Jordan River into the land I
am giving them. . . . Be strong and courageous,
for you are the one who will lead these people to
possess all the land I swore to their ancestors I would
give them."   JOSHUA 1:1-2, 6

My life is worth nothing to me unless I use it for
finishing the work assigned me by the Lord Jesus.

ACTS 20:24

Joshua knew for certain that God was calling him to
lead Israel into the Promised Land. He was sure God
would give them victory. But how can *you* know when
God is calling you to an important task? How can you
be certain? The first thing to remember is that you
don't decide when you are called—God does. Joshua
didn't choose to be Israel's leader. He was swept along
with the rest of the Israelites in their desert wander-
ings and suddenly found himself being nominated for
a leadership position. Joshua had been living faithfully
for God, diligently developing his military skills, and
allowing himself to be mentored by Moses and tested
with responsibilities. He knew he couldn't fulfill God's
call with just his own wits or strength. His biggest decision wasn't whether he should be the army's commander but whether God wanted the army to fight.

When Joshua became convinced that God would lead
the army, he knew he couldn't lose. God was in it, and
Joshua was the logical choice as commander—the call
became clear. You don't need to worry about *how* God
will call you. Instead, you should concentrate on *why*
God would call you. A humble heart and consistent
obedience are two characteristics that will help you be
sure of God's call.

DIVINE PROMISE

AS FOR ME, I LOOK TO THE LORD FOR HELP.
I WAIT CONFIDENTLY FOR GOD TO SAVE ME,
AND MY GOD WILL CERTAINLY HEAR ME.
Micah 7:7

Balance

MY QUESTION *for* GOD

*How do I live a balanced life? I can't seem to get
everything done.*

A MOMENT *with* GOD

Jesus replied, "You must love the Lord your God with
all your heart, all your soul, and all your mind. This
is the first and greatest commandment. A second is
equally important: 'Love your neighbor as yourself.'
The entire law and all the demands of the prophets
are based on these two commandments."

MATTHEW 22:37-40

For everything there is a season, a time for every
activity under heaven.   ECCLESIASTES 3:1

I brought glory to you here on earth by completing
the work you gave me to do. Now, Father, bring me
into the glory we shared before the world began.

JOHN 17:4-5

*L*iving a balanced life means you honor God, others,
and yourself with the way you use your gifts and spend
your time and resources. It's easy to let your life get
out of balance by overemphasizing one aspect of your
responsibilities at the cost of others. God assures you
that there is a time for everything, and there is time for
everything he calls you to do. Jesus, despite his power
and the needs of those around him, left much undone;
yet he completed everything God had given him to do.
You will find true peace and contentment when you realize you don't have to do everything, just those things
God created you to do. You will find balance when
you know that in God's eyes you have done what you
need to do.

DIVINE PROMISE

ALL OF YOU TOGETHER ARE CHRIST'S BODY,
AND EACH OF YOU IS A PART OF IT.
1 Corinthians 12.27

Boredom

How should I deal with boredom?

Imitate God, therefore, in everything you do. . . .
Live a life filled with love, following the example
of Christ.   Ephesians 5:1-2

Don't look out only for your own interests, but take
an interest in others, too.   Philippians 2:4

The dictionary defines boredom as being weary with
tedious dullness. It might come from doing the same
thing over and over or doing work with no apparent
purpose or doing nothing for too long. Many people
with hectic schedules say, "I'd love to be bored for a
while." But there's a difference between boredom and
rest. We all need rest, but we don't need boredom.
Boredom is dangerous because it signifies lack of purpose and passion for anything meaningful. The antidote to boredom is finding something purposeful and
significant to do. God has a purpose for you, and finding that purpose is a divine moment. From that time
on, you will never be bored! Start by volunteering in a
ministry at your local church, or find a hobby that helps
you develop a skill. Then you will have something to
look forward to each day. The fire of passionate living
will ignite in your heart, and other people will be attracted to your enthusiasm.

DIVINE PROMISE

LET'S NOT GET TIRED OF DOING WHAT IS
GOOD. AT JUST THE RIGHT TIME WE WILL REAP
A HARVEST OF BLESSING IF WE DON'T GIVE UP.

Galatians 6:9

Brokenness

MY QUESTION *for* GOD

How can brokenness be a good thing?

A MOMENT *with* GOD

The sacrifice you desire is a broken spirit. You will
not reject a broken and repentant heart, O God.

PSALM 51:17

He heals the brokenhearted and bandages
their wounds.

PSALM 147:3

Brokenness is the awareness of your full dependence
on God. It signifies the breaking of your pride and self-
sufficiency. Brokenness often comes through circumstances that overwhelm you or through sin that reduces
you to nothing. You realize that the only way out of
your mess is through God's help. Those who are open
about their brokenness are often influential in helping
others. If you have been broken, allow God to use your
experience to help others overcome their struggles.

DIVINE PROMISE

THE LORD IS CLOSE TO THE BROKENHEARTED; HE RESCUES THOSE WHOSE SPIRITS ARE CRUSHED. *Psalm 34:18*

Brokenness

MY QUESTION *for* GOD

What does brokenness look like?

A MOMENT *with* GOD

David confessed to Nathan, "I have sinned against the LORD." Nathan replied, "Yes, but the LORD has forgiven you, and you won't die for this sin."

2 SAMUEL 12:13

Have mercy on me, O God, because of your unfailing love. Because of your great compassion, blot out the stain of my sins. Wash me clean from my guilt. Purify me from my sin. For I recognize my rebellion; it haunts me day and night. Against you, and you alone, have I sinned; I have done what is evil in your sight. You will be proved right in what you say, and your judgment against me is just.   PSALM 51:1-4

David was guilty of adultery with Bathsheba as well as the murder of her husband, Uriah. It doesn't get much worse than that. When the prophet Nathan confronted David with his sin, we get a picture of what brokenness should accomplish (see 2 Samuel 12). David didn't run from God. He didn't make excuses for his failure. He didn't give in to despair. Instead, he acknowledged God's justice and his own need for forgiveness. Then he cast himself on God's mercy. David recorded his heartfelt confession in Psalm 51. It is through brokenness that you are best able to experience God's mercy and forgiveness.

Peter said, "Man, I don't know what you are talking about." And immediately, while he was still speaking, the rooster crowed. At that moment the Lord turned and looked at Peter. Suddenly, the Lord's words flashed through Peter's mind: "Before the rooster crows tomorrow morning, you will deny three times that you even know me." And Peter left the courtyard, weeping bitterly.   LUKE 22:60-62

After breakfast Jesus asked Simon Peter, "Simon son of John, do you love me more than these?" "Yes, Lord," Peter replied, "you know I love you."   JOHN 21:15

After Peter denied Jesus, his spirit was broken. But when Jesus appeared to him after his resurrection, he restored Peter. He gave Peter the opportunity to unsay his denial by reaffirming his love. This speaks volumes to us about offering those who are broken another opportunity to start over again, to wipe their slate clean. If we come alongside those who are broken by failure, we can open the way for a divine moment when God restores and heals them.

DIVINE PROMISE

THE SACRIFICE YOU DESIRE IS A BROKEN
SPIRIT. YOU WILL NOT REJECT A BROKEN AND
REPENTANT HEART, O GOD.   *Psalm 51:17*

Burnout

MY QUESTION *for* GOD

*I'm burning the candle at both ends. How do I find the
strength to keep going when it seems I have nothing left?*

A MOMENT *with* GOD

When David and his men were in the thick of battle,
David became weak and exhausted.   2 SAMUEL 21:15

I am exhausted and completely crushed. My groans
come from an anguished heart.   PSALM 38:8

Only in returning to me and resting in me will
you be saved. In quietness and confidence is
your strength.   ISAIAH 30:15

Come to me, all of you who are weary and carry
heavy burdens, and I will give you rest. . . . You will
find rest for your souls.   MATTHEW 11:28-29

He gives power to the weak and strength to the
powerless. Even youths will become weak and tired,
and young men will fall in exhaustion. But those who
trust in the LORD will find new strength. They will

soar high on wings like eagles. They will run and not
grow weary. They will walk and not faint.

ISAIAH 40:29-31

*B*urnout is an overwhelming exhaustion and inability
to push on, usually brought about by too much stress.
We all experience times of burnout, when we feel
tapped out emotionally, mentally, physically, and spiritually. In our fast-paced, 24-7 world, it isn't surprising
that we become quickly exhausted. Because burnout
is so draining and paralyzing, you need to take care of
your body and mind by eating right, exercising, and
getting enough sleep and relaxation. One of the best
ways to reduce burnout is to take time out to be close
to God. When you draw close to him, you can tap into
his power, strength, peace, protection, and love. This
will give you the strength to persevere through even
the worst times of burnout.

DIVINE PROMISE

THE LORD IS MY SHEPHERD; I HAVE ALL THAT
I NEED. HE LETS ME REST IN GREEN MEADOWS;
HE LEADS ME BESIDE PEACEFUL STREAMS.
HE RENEWS MY STRENGTH. HE GUIDES ME
ALONG RIGHT PATHS, BRINGING HONOR TO
HIS NAME. *Psalm 23:1-3*

Business

MY QUESTION *for* GOD

Is God interested in my success in business?

A MOMENT *with* GOD

She goes to inspect a field and buys it; with her earnings she plants a vineyard.   PROVERBS 31:16

Do not defraud or rob your neighbor. Do not make your hired workers wait until the next day to receive their pay.   LEVITICUS 19:13

A Jew named Aquila . . . had recently arrived from Italy with his wife, Priscilla. . . . Paul lived and worked with them, for they were tentmakers just as he was.   ACTS 18:1-3

As slaves of Christ, do the will of God with all your heart. Work with enthusiasm, as though you were working for the Lord rather than for people.

EPHESIANS 6:6-7

God endorses hard work, ingenuity, fair business practices, and success. Paul, Aquila, and Priscilla were Christian leaders in both ministry and business and managed to do well at balancing both. The quality of your work and your enthusiasm for it reveal the nature of your commitment to Christ. Hard work done with excellence and integrity honors God and may bring material resources that can be used for God's glory. But hard work does not always lead to material success.

What is most important is that you do your work as though God were your boss. If you work to serve him, you will be successful in God's eyes.

DIVINE PROMISE

COMMIT YOUR ACTIONS TO THE LORD, AND YOUR PLANS WILL SUCCEED. *Proverbs 16:3*

Busyness

MY QUESTION *for* GOD

Does God want me to be busy all the time?

A MOMENT *with* GOD

We are merely moving shadows, and all our busy rushing ends in nothing. We heap up wealth, not knowing who will spend it.   PSALM 39:6

Enthusiasm without knowledge is no good; haste makes mistakes.   PROVERBS 19:2

You hoped for rich harvests, but they were poor. And when you brought your harvest home, I blew it away. Why? Because my house lies in ruins, says the LORD of Heaven's Armies, while all of you are busy building your own fine houses.   HAGGAI 1:9

He lets me rest in green meadows; he leads me beside peaceful streams.   PSALM 23:2

We often operate under the false assumption that being busy means being productive or that resting means being lazy. But it's possible to have unproductive activity and productive rest! The Bible points out many benefits of being busy, such as earning a living, providing for your family, and advancing God's kingdom. But being too busy can damage your relationships (with God and with others), cause burnout, or prevent you from focusing on your real priorities. As with anything you do, learning to strike a balance between working, having fun, and resting will allow you to be productive in all areas of life.

DIVINE PROMISE

JESUS SAID, "COME TO ME, ALL OF YOU WHO ARE WEARY AND CARRY HEAVY BURDENS, AND I WILL GIVE YOU REST. TAKE MY YOKE UPON YOU. LET ME TEACH YOU, BECAUSE I AM HUMBLE AND GENTLE AT HEART, AND YOU WILL FIND REST FOR YOUR SOULS." *Matthew 11:28-29*

Call of God

MY QUESTION *for* GOD

How do I know what my calling is?

A MOMENT *with* GOD

Your word is a lamp to guide my feet and a light for my path.   PSALM 119:105

𝒯he first step to discovering your calling is getting to know God better by reading his Word. As God communicates to you through the Bible, he will show you what he wants you to do and where he wants you to go.

God gave these four young men an unusual aptitude for understanding every aspect of literature and wisdom.   DANIEL 1:17

𝒢od has given every individual special aptitudes and abilities. These provide the biggest clue to understanding what God wants you to do. When he calls you to do something specific for him, he will almost always allow you to use your God-given gifts to get the job done. As you await his call, develop those special abilities and begin to use them. Strive to serve God, and live in ways that utilize your primary gifts. Then you will be prepared to hear God's call.

My life is worth nothing to me unless I use it for finishing the work assigned me by the Lord Jesus.

ACTS 20:24

𝒲hen God gives you a specific calling, it fills your thoughts and demands all your energy. You have a longing to pursue it wholeheartedly.

Let God transform you into a new person by changing the way you think. Then you will learn to know God's will for you.   ROMANS 12:2

When you let God transform you by the power of his Holy Spirit, he will literally begin to change your thoughts so that you will know what he wants you to do.

DIVINE PROMISE

GOD'S GIFTS AND HIS CALL CAN NEVER BE WITHDRAWN. *Romans 11:29*

Challenges

MY QUESTION *for* GOD

How do challenges shape my life?

A MOMENT *with* GOD

My ambition has always been to preach the Good News where the name of Christ has never been heard. . . . I have been following the plan spoken of in the Scriptures, where it says, "Those who have never been told about him will see, and those who have never heard of him will understand." In fact, my visit to you has been delayed so long because I have been preaching in these places. ROMANS 15:20-22

We think you ought to know, dear brothers and sisters, about the trouble we went through in the province of Asia. We were crushed and overwhelmed beyond our ability to endure, and we thought we would never live through it. In fact, we expected to die. But as a result, we stopped relying on ourselves and learned to rely only on God, who raises the dead. And he did rescue us.   2 CORINTHIANS 1:8-10

*P*aul's goal to preach the gospel in new places continually brought him new challenges. These challenges caused greater growth in his relationship with God. God has called you to do something for him. Find out what it is, and accept the challenge of stepping out in faith to do it. Challenges force you to follow God's leading into uncharted waters so that you learn to trust him. Then you can accomplish his unique purpose for you. It is truly a divine moment when you realize exactly what God wants you to do, and it is often through challenges that God makes his plan clear to you.

DIVINE PROMISE

BE STRONG AND COURAGEOUS, AND DO THE WORK. DON'T BE AFRAID OR DISCOURAGED, FOR THE LORD GOD . . . IS WITH YOU. HE WILL NOT FAIL YOU OR FORSAKE YOU.   *1 Chronicles 28:20*

Change

MY QUESTION *for* GOD

When is change positive?

A MOMENT *with* GOD

Don't copy the behavior and customs of this world,
but let God transform you into a new person by
changing the way you think. Then you will learn to
know God's will for you, which is good and pleasing
and perfect.   ROMANS 12:2

Now repent of your sins and turn to God, so that
your sins may be wiped away.   ACTS 3:19

Change is one of the great constants of life. Whether
because of the gradual passage of time or cataclysmic
moments of trauma, change happens to everything and
everyone. People change, relationships change, jobs
change, technology changes—indeed, life itself can
be described as a process of continual change. Some
changes are positive: making a new friend, moving
into a new house, receiving a financial windfall. Other
changes are negative: suffering a tragic loss, getting laid
off from a job, surviving the upheaval of a natural disaster. Either way, change is stressful. The Bible offers two
truths about change. The first is that despite the changing world around us, God is changeless and dependable.
The second is that God wants an inner change of heart,
called repentance, that produces an outward change of
lifestyle, called obedience. When you change your heart,
you will change your life forever.

DIVINE PROMISE

I AM CERTAIN THAT GOD, WHO BEGAN THE
GOOD WORK WITHIN YOU, WILL CONTINUE
HIS WORK UNTIL IT IS FINALLY FINISHED ON
THE DAY WHEN CHRIST JESUS RETURNS.

Philippians 1:6

Change

MY QUESTION *for* GOD

Can Jesus change even the worst people on earth?

A MOMENT *with* GOD

The Lord said, "Go over to Straight Street, to the
house of Judas. When you get there, ask for a man
from Tarsus named Saul. . . . I have shown him a
vision of a man named Ananias coming in and laying
hands on him so he can see again." "But Lord,"
exclaimed Ananias, "I've heard many people talk
about the terrible things this man has done to the
believers in Jerusalem! And he is authorized by the
leading priests to arrest everyone who calls upon your
name." But the Lord said, "Go, for Saul is my chosen
instrument to take my message to the Gentiles and to
kings, as well as to the people of Israel."   ACTS 9:11-15

Think of the cruelest, most evil person you know. Are
you praying for that person? Is it possible for the Lord
to change that terrible person into an on-fire believer

in Jesus? If you doubt that he can, remember Saul. He was a mass murderer, inflicting enormous suffering on Christians and wreaking havoc in the early church. How could God save a wretch like that? But he did. Not only did Saul become the apostle Paul, but God also spoke through him to write many of the books in the New Testament. Who would have believed it? But it happened. The next time you find yourself hating that wicked person, stop and change directions. Pray for him or her instead. Then don't be surprised if you see God begin to change that person.

DIVINE PROMISE

ANYONE WHO BELONGS TO CHRIST HAS BECOME A NEW PERSON. THE OLD LIFE IS GONE; A NEW LIFE HAS BEGUN! *2 Corinthians 5:17*

Character

MY QUESTION *for* GOD

Why does my character matter?

A MOMENT *with* GOD

Suppose a certain man is righteous and does what is just and right. . . . He does not commit adultery. . . . He is a merciful creditor. . . . He does not rob the poor but instead gives food to the hungry and provides clothes for the needy. He grants loans without interest, stays away from injustice, is honest

and fair when judging others, and faithfully obeys
my decrees and regulations. Anyone who does
these things is just and will surely live, says the
Sovereign LORD.   . EZEKIEL 18:5-9

The Holy Spirit produces this kind of fruit in our
lives: love, joy, peace, patience, kindness, goodness,
faithfulness, gentleness, and self-control.

GALATIANS 5:22-23

That elusive thing called character is who you really
are—the sum total of everything that distinguishes you
as a person from everyone else. Your reputation—what
other people say about you—is often a good indication
of your character. If you overheard two people talking
about you, what would they be saying? Character is
what you are, but it is also what you desire to become.
Ultimately, your character is the mark you make on
the world. If you are striving for good character—
better yet, for godly character—you are working toward moral excellence. Think of all the areas in your
life, such as your career or hobbies, in which you've
worked hard to develop excellence. Doesn't it make
sense, then, to work hard at becoming morally excellent and mastering the things that really matter, such as
integrity, kindness, love, and faithfulness? You can do
that by asking God to work through you as you relate
to others.

DIVINE PROMISE

GOD IS WORKING IN YOU, GIVING YOU
THE DESIRE AND THE POWER TO DO WHAT
PLEASES HIM. *Philippians 2:13*

Character

MY QUESTION *for* GOD

Why does character building have to be so hard?

A MOMENT *with* GOD

Until the time came to fulfill his dreams, the LORD
tested Joseph's character.   PSALM 105:19

Dear brothers and sisters, when troubles come your
way, consider it an opportunity for great joy. For you
know that when your faith is tested, your endurance
has a chance to grow. So let it grow, for when your
endurance is fully developed, you will be perfect and
complete, needing nothing.   JAMES 1:2-4

Endurance develops strength of character, and
character strengthens our confident hope of salvation.

ROMANS 5:4

*I*t is a basic principle of life that adversity produces
strength. Just as your muscles grow only when stretched
to their limit, so your character grows only when the
pressures of life push against it and test its strength. Developing strong character, therefore, is a process that

takes time and constant attention. Your muscles will get flabby if you stop exercising. Likewise, your character will get soft if you stop working on it. It may not be easy, but it is only through hard work that you will achieve great accomplishment and the sense of satisfaction that goes along with it. The pressure from pain, trials, and temptations will refine you so that over time you will be better equipped and more experienced to deal with them. Character building is hard work that always pays off, both now and for eternity.

Divine Promise

THE MORE YOU GROW LIKE THIS, THE MORE PRODUCTIVE AND USEFUL YOU WILL BE IN YOUR KNOWLEDGE OF OUR LORD JESUS CHRIST. *2 Peter 1:8*

Church

My Question *for* God

Do I really need to go to church?

A Moment *with* God

The church is his body; it is made full and complete by Christ, who fills all things everywhere with himself. EPHESIANS 1:23

The human body has many parts, but the many parts make up one whole body. So it is with the body of Christ.

1 CORINTHIANS 12:12

Let us not neglect our meeting together, as some people do, but encourage one another, especially now that the day of his return is drawing near.

HEBREWS 10:25

*T*ogether all believers make up God's family, and it is only by meeting together that you can bond. One purpose of the church is to equip God's people to do God's work and to encourage them in their faith. The church is where Christians learn to work together in unity, reconciling differences among themselves in a way that is only possible through Christ and his Spirit. When you meet together with other believers, you build each other up and help each other. The church needs you because the body of Christ is not complete unless you are there. While God is present everywhere, he creates many divine moments where believers gather to worship him, serve him, and learn about him.

DIVINE PROMISE

UPON THIS ROCK I WILL BUILD MY CHURCH, AND ALL THE POWERS OF HELL WILL NOT CONQUER IT. *Matthew 16:18*

Commitment

What is the cost of being committed to God?

A Moment *with* God

If you want to be my disciple, you must hate everyone
else by comparison—your father and mother, wife
and children, brothers and sisters—yes, even your
own life. Otherwise, you cannot be my disciple. And
if you do not carry your own cross and follow me,
you cannot be my disciple. But don't begin until you
count the cost. For who would begin construction of
a building without first calculating the cost to see if
there is enough money to finish it?   Luke 14:26-28

Is Jesus really telling us to turn our back on our family? Of course not! We can understand the apparent
harshness of his words only when we grasp the nature
of commitment. Jesus wants you to see that commitment is exclusive and costly. A person fully devoted to
becoming a professional musician cannot also be fully
dedicated to becoming a professional athlete without
compromising his commitment to one profession or
the other. In the same way, your commitment to Jesus
must become the central and dominating commitment
of your life; all other relationships and pursuits must be
considered in light of your commitment to him. When
you are fully committed to Jesus, you will make your
financial decisions based on biblical principles instead
of simply buying whatever you want. You may make

sacrifices to help a needy family, even though it puts additional strain on your own family. Think about your commitment to God. Is it diluted by overcommitment to other people or activities? Evaluate each of your commitments by asking yourself, "Is this worthy of my time and energy in light of my complete commitment to Jesus?"

DIVINE PROMISE

IF WE ARE FAITHFUL TO THE END, . . . WE WILL SHARE IN ALL THAT BELONGS TO CHRIST.
Hebrews 3:14

Communication

MY QUESTION *for* GOD

Why is communication with God so important when he knows what I'm thinking anyway?

A MOMENT *with* GOD

You can be sure of this: The LORD set apart the godly for himself. The LORD will answer when I call to him.   PSALM 4:3

Because of Christ and our faith in him, we can now come boldly and confidently into God's presence.

EPHESIANS 3:12

The LORD is close to all who call on him, yes, to all who call on him in truth. He grants the desires of

those who fear him; he hears their cries for help and
rescues them. PSALM 145:18-19

Let us go right into the presence of God with sincere
hearts fully trusting him. HEBREWS 10:22

Devote yourselves to prayer with an alert mind and a
thankful heart. COLOSSIANS 4:2

O God, you are my God; I earnestly search for you.
My soul thirsts for you; my whole body longs for
you in this parched and weary land where there is
no water. PSALM 63:1

Communication is easier today than ever before. We
have cell phones, the Internet—cell phones with Internet—fax machines, e-mail, GPS tracking systems,
telephones, and walkie-talkies. Why? Because communication is important. We keep in touch because
it is vital to the quality and success of our relationships, whether with our wife, friends, family members, or business partners. The same principal applies
to your relationship with God. You must find ways to
communicate with him and learn to listen as he communicates with you. Only then will you experience a
breakthrough in your spiritual life. The more time you
spend communicating with God, the closer and more
successful your relationship with him will be. When
was the last time you felt in touch with God? Do you
need to spend more time communicating with him?

Communication

MY QUESTION *for* GOD

How can I know when God is speaking to me?

A MOMENT *with* GOD

My sheep listen to my voice; I know them, and they
follow me.   JOHN 10:27

Anyone who belongs to God listens gladly to the
words of God.   JOHN 8:47

The best way to be certain you are hearing God's
voice is to know God. If you don't know God, how
can you recognize his voice?

Before daybreak the next morning, Jesus got up and
went out to an isolated place to pray.   MARK 1:35

Be still, and know that I am God! I will be honored
by every nation. I will be honored throughout
the world.   PSALM 46:10

*P*rayer is talking to God and building a relationship with him. Good conversation also includes listening, so you must allow God to speak to you. Only when you hear God can he make his wisdom and resources available to you. Sometimes you must spend time in his presence without feeling the need to verbalize your prayers. Just begin to think about God. Then listen and be ready to hear him speak to your heart and mind. As you meditate, you will learn to distinguish between your own thoughts and any ideas prompted by God.

The word of God is alive and powerful. It is sharper than the sharpest two-edged sword, cutting between soul and spirit, between joint and marrow. It exposes our innermost thoughts and desires. HEBREWS 4:12

*J*ust as a piano is tuned using a standard tuning fork, so you can only get in tune with God by comparing yourself to the unchanging standards for living found in the Bible. As God communicates to you through his Word, you will begin to hear or discern just what he wants of you. As your spiritual hearing is fine-tuned, you will become a better listener, better able to hear God when he calls you to a certain task that he has reserved just for you. Would God say that you are a good listener?

Who can know the Lord's thoughts? Who knows enough to teach him? But we understand these things, for we have the mind of Christ.

1 CORINTHIANS 2:16

When you become a Christian, the Holy Spirit helps you understand the mind of Christ. He gives you guidance, wisdom, and discernment that is not available to those who don't know the Lord.

DIVINE PROMISE

DON'T WORRY ABOUT ANYTHING; INSTEAD,
PRAY ABOUT EVERYTHING. TELL GOD WHAT
YOU NEED, AND THANK HIM FOR ALL HE
HAS DONE. THEN YOU WILL EXPERIENCE
GOD'S PEACE.   *Philippians 4:6-7*

Competition

MY QUESTION *for* GOD

How can I use my competitive nature for God?

A MOMENT *with* GOD

Whatever I am now, it is all because God poured out his special favor on me—and not without results. For I have worked harder than any of the other apostles; yet it was not I but God who was working through me by his grace.   1 CORINTHIANS 15:10

Athletes cannot win the prize unless they follow the rules.   2 TIMOTHY 2:5

Work willingly at whatever you do, as though you were working for the Lord rather than for people.

COLOSSIANS 3:23

$\mathcal{I}$t's a dog-eat-dog world out there." "Winner take all." "Nice guys finish last." "Move up or move over." "Winning isn't everything—it's the only thing." These are the slogans of a world driven by competition. When properly focused, competition can bring out the best in you. But when infected with selfish ambition and pride, it can destroy relationships and corrode your heart. God's Word encourages a balanced and healthy understanding of competition. Let your competitive nature drive you to improve yourself personally and sharpen your spiritual skills. The apostle Paul is a good example of a godly person who used his competitive nature in God's service to reach people with the Good News about Jesus and to plant churches throughout the world. There's nothing wrong with a competitive nature. Just make sure you are not competing for the wrong things with the wrong motives. Keep your drive for competition in check so you don't hurt someone in the process of trying to win. As a Christian, you are called to work hard to do your best, not to compete against others simply to beat them. If beating others is your only goal, you honor only yourself; you have taken your eyes off God. If doing your best is your goal, you honor the God who created you.

DIVINE PROMISE

THANK GOD! HE GIVES US VICTORY OVER SIN AND DEATH THROUGH OUR LORD JESUS CHRIST. *1 Corinthians 15:57*

Compromise

How can I live in today's culture without compromising my convictions?

Daniel was determined not to defile himself by eating the food and wine given to them by the king. He asked the chief of staff for permission not to eat these unacceptable foods. . . . "Please test us for ten days on a diet of vegetables and water," Daniel said. . . . The attendant agreed to Daniel's suggestion. . . . At the end of the ten days, Daniel and his three friends looked healthier and better nourished than the young men who had been eating the food assigned by the king.   DANIEL 1:8, 12, 14-15

Be very careful never to make a treaty with the people who live in the land where you are going. If you do, you will follow their evil ways and be trapped.   EXODUS 34:12

There is a time to compromise and a time to stand firm. When the forces of evil tempt you to give up your convictions, you cannot budge. To compromise God's truth, God's ways, or God's Word is to negotiate with that which is unholy. The test of acceptable compromise is simple: Can you reach an agreement that satisfies both parties without sacrificing anyone's morals? If you give up godliness in exchange for anything else, it's a bad bargain. You lose and Satan wins. You can experience a divine moment if you refuse to compromise your convictions, and you will feel a sense of peace that you have done the right thing.

DIVINE PROMISE

PUT ON ALL OF GOD'S ARMOR SO THAT YOU WILL BE ABLE TO STAND FIRM AGAINST ALL STRATEGIES OF THE DEVIL. *Ephesians 6:11*

Confession

MY QUESTION *for* GOD

Why is confession essential in my relationship with God?

A MOMENT *with* GOD

Finally, I confessed all my sins to you and stopped trying to hide my guilt. I said to myself, "I will confess my rebellion to the LORD." And you forgave me! All my guilt is gone.   PSALM 32:5

If we confess our sins to him, he is faithful and just to forgive us our sins and to cleanse us from all wickedness.   1 JOHN 1:9

Everyone who acknowledges me publicly here on earth, I will also acknowledge before my Father in heaven.   MATTHEW 10:32

Confess your sins to each other and pray for each
other so that you may be healed. The earnest prayer
of a righteous person has great power and produces
wonderful results.   JAMES 5:16

*C*onfession is admitting to other people or to God that
you are guilty of some wrong. When you have to acknowledge the ugliness of your own sin, it can be em-
barrassing and even painful. Perhaps the embarrassment
comes from letting others see deeply into your heart or
from being vulnerable to ridicule. But confession is a
necessary part of knowing God, receiving his forgiveness, being released from guilt, and finding a new start.
Confession is essential to knowing God because it is only
through humility that you can establish honesty and trust
with him. Confession is essential to being freed from
the eternal consequences of sin because it brings about
God's forgiveness. Another form of confession—when
you profess your allegiance to God—is also essential in
your relationship with God because it gives you the courage to stand up for your faith when it is tested. It is only
through confession that you maintain an open line of
communication with God, putting yourself in the position to experience divine moments with him.

DIVINE PROMISE

IF YOU CONFESS WITH YOUR MOUTH THAT
JESUS IS LORD AND BELIEVE IN YOUR HEART
THAT GOD RAISED HIM FROM THE DEAD, YOU
WILL BE SAVED. *Romans 10:9*

Conflict

MY QUESTION *for* GOD

*Conflict is unavoidable. Is it possible to honor God even
in conflict?*

A MOMENT *with* GOD

The sinful nature wants to do evil, which is just the
opposite of what the Spirit wants. And the Spirit
gives us desires that are the opposite of what the
sinful nature desires. These two forces are constantly
fighting each other, so you are not free to carry
out your good intentions. . . . But the Holy Spirit
produces this kind of fruit in our lives: love, joy,
peace, patience, kindness, goodness, faithfulness,
gentleness, and self-control.   GALATIANS 5:17, 22-23

You have heard the law that says, "Love your
neighbor" and hate your enemy. But I say, love your
enemies! Pray for those who persecute you! In that
way, you will be acting as true children of your
Father in heaven.   MATTHEW 5:43-45

*W*hen a ballplayer disagrees with an umpire's call,
a spectacular and entertaining argument sometimes
begins. Grown men stand toe-to-toe, faces beet red,
veins popping out on their necks as they shout at each
other; "I was safe!" "You were out!" "Safe!" "Out!"
Since people have differing opinions on everything
from sports to politics to religion, conflict seems to be
a given in human relationships. The Bible does not hide
from the issue of conflict, and it does not condemn

all conflict as sinful. From Moses to David to Jesus to Paul, all of the Bible's greatest figures found themselves in conflict. Disagreements happen. But the manner in which conflicts are resolved is extremely important. Conflict can become the catalyst for developing greater understanding, intimacy, and depth in your relationships, or it can cause anger, bitterness, and broken relationships. When you become a Christian, a new conflict begins inside of you, one that will be a lifelong battle: what you want versus what God wants. Fortunately, you also have the Holy Spirit living in you, and he gives you the tools you need to handle the inner conflict with your sinful nature as well as conflict with others. Over time, you will learn to turn arguments into peace, anger into patience, rage into gentleness, and sinful thoughts and actions into self-control. Even when you're in the midst of a conflict, a divine moment can occur when others are able to see God rather than anger in you.

DIVINE PROMISE

GOD BLESSES THOSE WHO WORK FOR PEACE,
FOR THEY WILL BE CALLED THE CHILDREN
OF GOD.   *Matthew 5:9*

Conflict

MY QUESTION *for* GOD

What are some ways to resolve conflict?

A MOMENT *with* GOD

"Let's not allow this conflict to come between us or our herdsmen. . . . Take your choice of any section of the land you want, and we will separate." GENESIS 13:8-9

*R*esolving conflict takes initiative; someone must make the first move. Abram deferred to Lot, putting family peace above personal desires.

Isaac's men then dug another well, but again there was a dispute over it. . . . Isaac moved on and dug another well. This time there was no dispute over it.

GENESIS 26:21-22

*R*esolving conflict takes humility, persistence, and a preference for peace over personal victory.

That was the beginning of a long war between those who were loyal to Saul and those loyal to David.

2 SAMUEL 3:1

*R*esolving conflict involves compromise. The two sides must try to find common ground that is bigger than their differences. If neither side is willing to take the initiative or show the necessary humility to seek common ground, the conflict could result in broken friendships, broken marriages, even all-out war.

Even to have such lawsuits with one another is a defeat for you. Why not just accept the injustice and leave it at that? Why not let yourselves be cheated?

1 CORINTHIANS 6:7

*Y*ou might have to give up your rights in order to re-solve a conflict of interest, especially when it involves other Christians.

I pray that they will all be one, just as you and I are one—as you are in me, Father.   JOHN 17:21

*P*raying for peace and unity with others helps resolve conflict because you are seeking the help of the great Peacemaker.

Barnabas . . . wanted to take along John Mark. But Paul disagreed strongly. . . . Their disagreement was so sharp that they separated.   ACTS 15:37-39

*C*onflict begins when two people with opposing viewpoints are not willing to find common ground. Sometimes differences of opinion are so strong that no resolution is possible and a parting of ways is necessary. But even in these situations, God can use conflict to accomplish his will.

A servant of the Lord must not quarrel but must be kind to everyone, be able to teach, and be patient with difficult people. Gently instruct those who oppose the truth.   2 TIMOTHY 2:24-25

*W*hen someone disagrees with what you are saying, maintain a gracious, gentle, and patient attitude instead of becoming angry or defensive.

You have heard the law that says, "Love your neighbor" and hate your enemy. But I say, love your enemies! Pray for those who persecute you! In that way, you will be acting as true children of your Father in heaven.

MATTHEW 5:43-45

*H*uman nature wants to love friends and hate enemies. But Jesus taught a new perspective—the only way to resolve some conflicts is to reach out in love to your enemy. This kind of love can actually turn some enemies into friends.

If another believer sins against you, go privately and point out the offense. If the other person listens and confesses it, you have won that person back. But if you are unsuccessful, take one or two others with you and go back again, so that everything you say may be confirmed by two or three witnesses. If the person still refuses to listen, take your case to the church.

MATTHEW 18:15-17

*J*esus outlines a three-step process for confronting and resolving major conflicts between believers. This biblical solution begins with private confrontation.

DIVINE PROMISE

HE RANSOMS ME AND KEEPS ME SAFE FROM
THE BATTLE WAGED AGAINST ME, THOUGH
MANY STILL OPPOSE ME.   *Psalm 55:18*

Conscience

MY QUESTION *for* GOD

How can I have a clear conscience?

A MOMENT *with* GOD

Learn to know the God of your ancestors intimately.
Worship and serve him with your whole heart and
a willing mind. For the LORD sees every heart and
knows every plan and thought.   1 CHRONICLES 28:9

May the words of my mouth and the meditation of my
heart be pleasing to you, O LORD, my rock and my
redeemer.   PSALM 19:14

My conscience is clear, but that doesn't prove I'm
right. It is the Lord himself who will examine me
and decide.   1 CORINTHIANS 4:4

*W*hen your motives are selfish or impure, it is only a
matter of time before your actions become selfish and
impure. God is far more concerned about the condition
of your heart than he is with your external behavior.
Your behavior always flows from what is in your heart,
not the other way around. Remember that God alone

knows your heart. You may be able to fool others and even yourself, but you can't fool God. Welcome his examination. Then, like Paul, you can say that your conscience is clear. And when your conscience is clear, your heart will be open to God doing a great work in you and through you.

DIVINE PROMISE

YOUR WORD IS A LAMP TO GUIDE MY FEET AND A LIGHT FOR MY PATH.   *Psalm 119:105*

Convictions

MY QUESTION *for* GOD

How do convictions strengthen my faith?

A MOMENT *with* GOD

Daniel was determined not to defile himself by eating the food and wine given to them by the king. He asked the chief of staff for permission not to eat these unacceptable foods.   DANIEL 1:8

This will continue until we all come to such unity in our faith and knowledge of God's Son that we will be mature in the Lord, measuring up to the full and complete standard of Christ. Then we will no longer be immature like children. We won't be tossed and blown about by every wind of new teaching. We will not be influenced when people try to trick us with lies so clever they sound like the truth. Instead, we will speak the truth in love, growing in every way more and more like Christ, who is the head of his body, the church.   EPHESIANS 4:13-15

*H*aving convictions means more than just having beliefs; it means being committed to your beliefs. What you think, say, and do shows the strength of your convictions. For example, when you believe Jesus Christ is who he claims to be, then out of this belief should come the conviction to live according to his teachings. Convictions prepare you to effectively live a life of faith and to defend your faith when necessary. Conviction can also refer to the work of the Holy Spirit in your heart, when he tells you what is right and wrong. Without the Holy Spirit convicting your heart, you would be unprepared to face temptation and might easily give in when confronted by someone with stronger convictions. Convictions hold you steady on the path of life and help you faithfully live out your belief in God in practical ways. Keep your convictions firm, and your life as a Christian will be full of divine moments.

DIVINE PROMISE

LET THE HOLY SPIRIT GUIDE YOUR LIVES. THEN YOU WON'T BE DOING WHAT YOUR SINFUL NATURE CRAVES. THE SINFUL NATURE WANTS TO DO EVIL, WHICH IS JUST THE OPPOSITE OF WHAT THE SPIRIT WANTS. AND THE SPIRIT GIVES US DESIRES THAT ARE THE OPPOSITE OF WHAT THE SINFUL NATURE DESIRES.

Galatians 5:16-17

Convictions

What are some basic convictions I should have as a Christian?

A MOMENT *with* GOD

God has given both his promise and his oath. These two things are unchangeable because it is impossible for God to lie. Therefore, we who have fled to him for refuge can have great confidence as we hold to the hope that lies before us.   HEBREWS 6:18

This truth gives them confidence that they have eternal life, which God—who does not lie— promised them before the world began.   TITUS 1:2

God always keeps his promises. He cannot lie, so his Word is truth. You can trust what he says.

Then God gave the people all these instructions: "I am the LORD your God, who rescued you from the land of Egypt, the place of your slavery. You must not have any other god but me."   EXODUS 20:1-3

God must be the first priority in your life. When he is, you will see things from his perspective, which will change the way you act and think.

If you confess with your mouth that Jesus is Lord and believe in your heart that God raised him from the dead, you will be saved.   ROMANS 10:9

Anyone who belongs to Christ has become a new person. The old life is gone; a new life has begun!

2 CORINTHIANS 5:17

If we confess our sins to him, he is faithful and just to forgive us our sins and to cleanse us from all wickedness.

1 JOHN 1:9

*I*f you are truly sorry for your sins and confess them to God, and if you believe that God's Son, Jesus, died for you to take upon himself the punishment for sin you deserve, then God forgives you and gives you the gift of salvation. The moment you are saved, the Holy Spirit enters your heart and begins transforming you into a new person from the inside out. Then you and everyone else will see that your life is different.

We will speak the truth in love, growing in every way more and more like Christ, who is the head of his body, the church.

EPHESIANS 4:15

*I*f you live by the truths in God's Word, you will become more and more like Jesus. This should be your primary goal.

Do not throw away this confident trust in the Lord. Remember the great reward it brings you!

HEBREWS 10:35

Blessed are those who trust in the LORD and have made the LORD their hope and confidence.

JEREMIAH 17:7

*T*rusting in the Lord brings great blessing and eternal rewards.

I am praying to you because I know you will answer, O God. Bend down and listen as I pray. PSALM 17:6

*G*od answers prayer.

I know the LORD is always with me. I will not be shaken, for he is right beside me. PSALM 16:8

*G*od is always with you.

I am convinced that nothing can ever separate us from God's love. Neither death nor life, neither angels nor demons, neither our fears for today nor our worries about tomorrow—not even the powers of hell can separate us from God's love. No power in the sky above or in the earth below—indeed, nothing in all creation will ever be able to separate us from the love of God that is revealed in Christ Jesus our Lord. ROMANS 8:38-39

*N*othing can separate you from God's love for you.

DIVINE PROMISE
LET THOSE WHO ARE WISE UNDERSTAND THESE
THINGS. LET THOSE WITH DISCERNMENT
LISTEN CAREFULLY. THE PATHS OF THE LORD
ARE TRUE AND RIGHT, AND RIGHTEOUS PEOPLE
LIVE BY WALKING IN THEM. BUT IN THOSE
PATHS SINNERS STUMBLE AND FALL.   *Hosea 14:9*

Courage

MY QUESTION *for* GOD

Why doesn't God take away my greatest fears?

A MOMENT *with* GOD

All the believers lifted their voices together in prayer
to God: " . . . . O Lord, hear their threats, and give
us, your servants, great boldness. . . . Stretch out
your hand with healing power; may miraculous signs
and wonders be done through the name of your holy
servant Jesus." After this prayer, the meeting place
shook, and they were all filled with the Holy Spirit.
Then they preached the word of God with boldness.

ACTS 4:24, 29-31

Having hope will give you courage.   JOB 11:18

The early church was constantly threatened with persecution. The believers did not pray for the threats to
be taken away but for the courage to face them. Sometimes God will remove the things that frighten you.

But more often the Holy Spirit gives you the boldness to turn those fears into opportunities for spiritual growth and sharing your faith. If God were to take away everything that frightens you, there would be no need for hope in your life. It is hope that helps you see beyond your immediate crisis and place your current problem, as well as your eternal future, in God's hands. When you are overwhelmed by the enormity of the problem facing you, let it be a divine moment of recognition that God is right by your side.

DIVINE PROMISE

BE STRONG AND COURAGEOUS! DO NOT BE AFRAID OR DISCOURAGED. FOR THE LORD YOUR GOD IS WITH YOU WHEREVER YOU GO. *Joshua 1:9*

Crisis

MY QUESTION *for* GOD

Can my response to a crisis reveal my faith in God?

A MOMENT *with* GOD

As Pharaoh approached, the people of Israel looked up and panicked when they saw the Egyptians overtaking them. They cried out to the LORD, and they said to Moses, "Why did you bring us out here to die in the wilderness? Weren't there enough graves for us in Egypt? What have you done to us? Why did you make us leave Egypt? Didn't we tell you this would happen while we were still in Egypt? We said, 'Leave us alone! Let us be slaves to the Egyptians. It's better to be a slave in Egypt than a corpse in the wilderness!'" But Moses told the people, "Don't be afraid. Just stand still and watch the LORD rescue you today. . . . The LORD himself will fight for you. Just stay calm."   EXODUS 14:10-14

*T*oo often a crisis exposes your unbelief and fear rather than your confidence and trust in God. The Israelites panicked when they saw Pharaoh's army approaching. In spite of everything they had seen the Lord do in Egypt, they did not trust him to deliver them this time. The army they could see seemed more powerful than the God they could not see. Their response to crisis teaches us that it is not enough simply to know about or even to witness God's mighty acts. You must allow God's faithfulness in the past to bolster your faith that God will deliver you from your present trials. Times of crisis can strengthen your character and allow God's transforming power to touch you more deeply. It doesn't matter what the cause or the magnitude of the crisis is; how you handle it and to whom you go for help are the keys to effectively getting through it. A crisis can raise questions about the presence of God and his role in the situation. The answers you find to those questions will reveal the strength of your faith.

DIVINE PROMISE

GOD IS OUR REFUGE AND STRENGTH, ALWAYS
READY TO HELP IN TIMES OF TROUBLE. SO WE
WILL NOT FEAR WHEN EARTHQUAKES COME
AND THE MOUNTAINS CRUMBLE INTO THE SEA.
LET THE OCEANS ROAR AND FOAM. LET THE
MOUNTAINS TREMBLE AS THE WATERS SURGE!

Psalm 46:1-3

Danger

MY QUESTION *for* GOD

What is one danger I face as a Christian?

A MOMENT *with* GOD

Dear children, keep away from anything that might
take God's place in your hearts.   1 JOHN 5:21

Stay alert! Watch out for your great enemy, the devil.
He prowls around like a roaring lion, looking for
someone to devour.   1 PETER 5:8

Temptation to do wrong is one danger you face constantly. When there's a dangerous curve in the road,
there's also usually a guardrail. The purpose of the
guardrail is not to inhibit your freedom to drive but
to save your life! It is an object of security and safety,
not an obstacle to your driving. In the same way, you
need a guardrail as you travel through life—not to inhibit your freedom but to help you avoid danger and

keep from going out of control. Your heart determines where you go because it affects your passions. If you don't guard your heart with God's Word and stay focused on the road God has put you on, you may have a terrible accident when temptation distracts you. Satan is constantly on the attack, trying to tempt you to sin against God. And you will give in sometimes—we all do. Don't throw caution to the wind, or you will likely give in to temptation at every turn and put yourself in danger of being completely ineffective for God. Instead, take caution so that you will be aware of temptation. Then you can recognize it, acknowledge it, and avoid it.

DIVINE PROMISE

THE WISE ARE CAUTIOUS AND AVOID DANGER;
FOOLS PLUNGE AHEAD WITH RECKLESS
CONFIDENCE.   *Proverbs 14:16*

Decisions

MY QUESTION *for* GOD

Do the decisions I make really matter that much?

A MOMENT *with* GOD

Commit your actions to the LORD, and your plans
will succeed.   PROVERBS 16:3

Oh, that we might know the LORD! Let us press on to know him. He will respond to us as surely as the arrival of dawn or the coming of rains in early spring.

HOSEA 6:3

My steps have stayed on your path; I have not wavered from following you.   PSALM 17.5

*M*aking right decisions is like hiking; each step puts you a little further down the path. Sometimes making the right decision simply means being faithful in little things. God's will for you is to read his Word, obey him, serve others, and do what is right. If you make decisions to do his will today, you can be sure that you will be doing his will twenty years from now. Then when you approach the end of your life, you will be able to finish well and leave behind a legacy of faithfulness.

DIVINE PROMISE

SEEK HIS WILL IN ALL YOU DO, AND HE WILL SHOW YOU WHICH PATH TO TAKE. *Proverbs 3:6*

Defeat

MY QUESTION *for* GOD

Why is it so important to try to defeat sin in my life?

A MOMENT *with* GOD

We use God's mighty weapons, not worldly weapons, to knock down the strongholds of human reasoning and to destroy false arguments.   2 CORINTHIANS 10:4

Stay alert! Watch out for your great enemy, the devil. He prowls around like a roaring lion, looking for someone to devour.   1 PETER 5:8

Do not let sin control the way you live; do not give in to sinful desires.   ROMANS 6:12

All have turned away; all have become corrupt. No one does good, not a single one!   PSALM 14:3

It's a nasty feeling to bite into an apple that looks good on the outside only to find that it's rotten on the inside. You spit it out because it repulses you. Sin works the same way. It can rot you from the inside, even if you look good on the outside. If left unchecked, sin can fester until it repulses God as well as other people when they see what's really inside you. A rotten apple can't be made whole again, but you can be. When you become a believer, a miraculous transformation takes place by the power of God. But Satan fights to keep you from believing that you've been truly transformed. You cannot afford to lose this battle or you will never live effectively for God. But you cannot fight Satan alone. You must use the armor God has given you to engage in this spiritual warfare. You must resist and fight against Satan and his forces of evil. Their goal is to conquer your heart and turn you against God. So you must fight with every bit of your strength and every available weapon God provides for you. You cannot totally defeat Satan while you live on this earth, but you can resist him and win the everyday battles against him. Remember that you will be victorious both in this life and in eternity.

DIVINE PROMISE

THE LORD IS FAITHFUL; HE WILL STRENGTHEN YOU AND GUARD YOU FROM THE EVIL ONE.
2 Thessalonians 3:3

Depression

MY QUESTION *for* GOD

Does feeling depressed mean something is wrong with my faith?

A MOMENT *with* GOD

I have told you these things so that you will be filled with my joy. Yes, your joy will overflow!   JOHN 15:11

Those who listen to instruction will prosper; those who trust the LORD will be joyful.   PROVERBS 16:20

God does not regard depression as sin, nor does he take it lightly. Rather, he responds with great tenderness, understanding, and compassion to those who suffer the darkness of depression. When you are depressed, the

Bible helps you recognize the lies of Satan, the temptations that might come your way, and the ways the devil fuels your depression by distracting you from God's promises and power. As you become more aware of these things, your perspective will begin to change. Develop the habit of seeking God and counting on his Word to be true; you will discover the encouragement you need.

Samson was now very thirsty, and he cried out to the LORD, "You have accomplished this great victory. . . . Must I now die of thirst and fall into the hands of these pagans?"   JUDGES 15:18

Elijah was afraid and fled for his life. . . . He sat down under a solitary broom tree and prayed that he might die.   1 KINGS 19:3-4

Even for the people of God, depression can follow great achievement or spiritual victory. After you experience such a high, it seems the only direction to go is down. If you recognize this, you won't be so surprised when you feel low after feeling on top of the world. This is normal. But beware of the tendency to neglect God after a spiritual victory. Instead, you should fill your heart and mind with God's Word, which will encourage you with God's love and care and keep you from sinking too low into depression.

DIVINE PROMISE

EVEN WHEN I WALK THROUGH THE DARKEST
VALLEY, I WILL NOT BE AFRAID, FOR YOU ARE
CLOSE BESIDE ME. YOUR ROD AND YOUR STAFF
PROTECT AND COMFORT ME.   *Psalm 23:4*

Desires

MY QUESTION *for* GOD

Is it okay to really want something?

A MOMENT *with* GOD

That night the LORD appeared to Solomon in a
dream, and God said, "What do you want? Ask, and
I will give it to you!"   1 KINGS 3:5

Hope deferred makes the heart sick, but a dream
fulfilled is a tree of life.   PROVERBS 13:12

I desire you more than anything on earth.   PSALM 73:25

LORD, we show our trust in you by obeying your
laws; our heart's desire is to glorify your name.

ISAIAH 26:8

If you look for me wholeheartedly, you will find me.

JEREMIAH 29:13

God created desire within you as a means of expressing yourself. Desires are good and healthy when they

are directed toward those things that are good and right and God-honoring. The same basic desire can be right or wrong, depending upon your motives and the object of your desire. For example, the desire to love a woman is healthy and right when it is directed toward your wife. But that same desire directed toward anyone you are not married to is adultery. The desire to lead an organization is healthy if your motive is to serve others, but it is unhealthy and wrong if your motive is to gain power or control over others. Your greatest desire must be for a relationship with God, which will influence all your other desires.

DIVINE PROMISE

I WILL GIVE YOU A NEW HEART, AND I WILL PUT A NEW SPIRIT IN YOU. I WILL TAKE OUT YOUR STONY, STUBBORN HEART AND GIVE YOU A TENDER, RESPONSIVE HEART. *Ezekiel 36:26*

Desires

MY QUESTION *for* GOD

How do I know if my desires are right or wrong?

A MOMENT *with* GOD

One day when Samson was in Timnah, one of the Philistine women caught his eye. When he returned home, he told his father and mother, "A young Philistine woman in Timnah caught my eye. I want

to marry her. Get her for me." His father and mother
objected. "Isn't there even one woman in our tribe
or among all the Israelites you could marry?" they
asked. "Why must you go to the pagan Philistines to
find a wife?" But Samson told his father, "Get her for
me! She looks good to me."   JUDGES 14:1-3

Fix your thoughts on what is true, and honorable,
and right, and pure, and lovely, and admirable. Think
about things that are excellent and worthy of praise.

PHILIPPIANS 4:8

Sinful desires are very powerful because they are
selfish. The desire to get what you want is so strong
that it can keep you from thinking straight. Samson
saw a beautiful woman and became consumed with
having her. It was as if his brain froze up; he didn't even
think about all the problems that would come from the
relationship. Like Samson, you can become so obsessed
with what you want that you forget to ask God if it is
what he wants. Make sure that the object of your desire
is consistent with God's Word, good for you, and not
harmful to others.

DIVINE CHALLENGE
IF YOU ARE WISE AND UNDERSTAND GOD'S
WAYS, PROVE IT BY LIVING AN HONORABLE
LIFE, DOING GOOD WORKS WITH THE
HUMILITY THAT COMES FROM WISDOM.
James 3:13

Discernment

MY QUESTION *for* GOD

What are the benefits of using discernment?

A MOMENT *with* GOD

I want you to understand what really matters, so that you may live pure and blameless lives until the day of Christ's return.   PHILIPPIANS 1:10

You need someone to teach you again the basic things about God's word. You are like babies who need milk and cannot eat solid food. For someone who lives on milk is still an infant and doesn't know how to do what is right. Solid food is for those who are mature, who through training have the skill to recognize the difference between right and wrong.   HEBREWS 5:12-14

Give me understanding and I will obey your instructions; I will put them into practice with all my heart.   PSALM 119:34

⟨⟩

Discernment comes from training yourself to distinguish between right and wrong by disciplining your conscience, mind, body, and senses. The Bible tells us that discernment is necessary to mature in your faith. In fact, it says that recognizing the difference between right and wrong is a developed skill. When you grow and mature in your faith, you will be able to recognize temptation before it overcomes you. You will learn to distinguish between truth and lies, between God's voice and other voices. When you know the Scriptures, you will be able to discern false teaching or if someone is using a passage of Scripture incorrectly. When you practice discernment and train yourself to detect right from wrong, you will be able to avoid the pitfalls and confusion that so many people fall into. Life works better when you live it the way God created it to work.

DIVINE PROMISE

MY CHILD, LISTEN TO WHAT I SAY, AND TREASURE MY COMMANDS. TUNE YOUR EARS TO WISDOM, AND CONCENTRATE ON UNDERSTANDING. CRY OUT FOR INSIGHT, AND ASK FOR UNDERSTANDING. SEARCH FOR THEM AS YOU WOULD FOR SILVER; SEEK THEM LIKE HIDDEN TREASURES. THEN YOU WILL UNDERSTAND WHAT IT MEANS TO FEAR THE LORD, AND YOU WILL GAIN KNOWLEDGE OF GOD. FOR THE LORD GRANTS WISDOM! FROM HIS MOUTH COME KNOWLEDGE AND UNDERSTANDING. *Proverbs 2:1-6*

Discipline

MY QUESTION *for* GOD

Could my troubles actually be a result of God disciplining me?

A MOMENT *with* GOD

My child, don't reject the LORD's discipline. . . . For the LORD corrects those he loves. PROVERBS 3:11-12

No one can tell [Jerusalem] anything; it refuses all correction. It does not trust in the LORD or draw near to its God.   ZEPHANIAH 3:2

*L*ike Jerusalem at the time of Zephaniah, you can stubbornly refuse to listen to God—or anyone else— and ignore the correction that could help you. When you get to that point, you are rebelling against God, and he may use adversity to get your attention and discipline you. Actually God's discipline is a divine moment of intervention; without it, you could continue to stray until you no longer hear his voice. Stay open to God's correction in your life, follow his directions for living found in the Bible, and listen carefully to the advice of godly people whom you respect. Be careful, however, not to immediately assume that your troubles (or the troubles someone else is experiencing) are the result of God's discipline. If you have been sincerely trying to follow God, chances are that there is another reason for your adversity.

DIVINE PROMISE

JOYFUL ARE THOSE YOU DISCIPLINE, LORD.
Psalm 94:12

Discipline

MY QUESTION *for* GOD

How can I discipline myself to obey God?

A MOMENT *with* GOD

Commit yourselves wholeheartedly to these words of
mine. Tie them to your hands and wear them on your
forehead as reminders. Teach them to your children.
Talk about them when you are at home and when you
are on the road, when you are going to bed and when
you are getting up. Write them on the doorposts of
your house.   DEUTERONOMY 11:18-20

It is difficult for most of us to make obedience to
God and his Word a daily habit. We are often tempted
to give in to those sins we most enjoy. Here are four
ways to help you cultivate the discipline of obedience: (1) Focus on Scripture; read and meditate on
it daily. (2) Teach Scripture to others, either adults or
children. This will help you to apply it to your own
life too. (3) Talk about what God is doing in your life
every chance you get. Tell others what God means to
you. (4) Keep a spiritual diary or journal; write down
Scripture passages and what you learn from them. If
you regularly follow these four steps, obedience will
naturally become a part of your everyday life. You will
even come to love the discipline of obeying God.

DIVINE PROMISE

EVEN MORE BLESSED ARE ALL WHO HEAR THE
WORD OF GOD AND PUT IT INTO PRACTICE.
Luke 11:28

Discontent

MY QUESTION *for* GOD

*Others say I don't seem happy anymore. What's wrong
with me?*

A MOMENT *with* GOD

Some people are always greedy for more, but the
godly love to give!   PROVERBS 21:26

Just as Death and Destruction are never satisfied, so
human desire is never satisfied.   PROVERBS 27:20

You want what you don't have, so you scheme and kill
to get it. You are jealous of what others have, but you
can't get it, so you fight and wage war to take it away
from them. Yet you don't have what you want because
you don't ask God for it.   JAMES 4:2

Those who live only to satisfy their own sinful nature
will harvest decay and death from that sinful nature.
But those who live to please the Spirit will harvest
everlasting life from the Spirit.   GALATIANS 6:8

𝒟eep within the human heart lurks the temptation to believe that there's more to life than what you are experiencing—or at least there should be something more. This feeling of discontent can gradually spread until you feel generally discontent with just about everything: You don't have enough money, your wife isn't the soul mate you hoped she would be, your church isn't meeting your needs, your job is less than inspiring, you can't do everything you want to do. If your wife, friends, or coworkers have recognized discontent in you and have pointed it out, you should take the cue and reverse course. Discontent is dangerous because it causes you to focus on yourself and on what you don't have. The antidote is to change your thinking. Whenever you find yourself thinking about what you don't have, stop and think about all the blessings you do have instead. Focus on Jesus and how he would serve those around you, and then begin doing the same. Your discontent will turn into true satisfaction. As you make God and others happy, you will find joy yourself.

DIVINE PROMISE

IF YOU TRY TO HANG ON TO YOUR LIFE, YOU WILL LOSE IT. BUT IF YOU GIVE UP YOUR LIFE FOR MY SAKE, YOU WILL SAVE IT. *Matthew 16:25*

Discouragement

MY QUESTION *for* GOD

How do I respond to feelings of discouragement?

A MOMENT *with* GOD

"I have had enough, LORD," [Elijah] said. "Take my life, for I am no better than my ancestors."   1 KINGS 19:4

Why am I discouraged? Why is my heart so sad? I will put my hope in God! I will praise him again—my Savior and my God! Now I am deeply discouraged, but I will remember you. . . . Each day the LORD pours his unfailing love upon me, and through each night I sing his songs, praying to God who gives me life.   PSALM 42:5-8

As soon as I pray, you answer me; you encourage me by giving me strength.   PSALM 138:3

From the depths of despair, O LORD, I call for your help.   PSALM 130:1

***

Discouragement settles in when you are facing a problem or task that seems overwhelming, if not impossible; when you've really messed up and feel embarrassed or ashamed; when you work your hardest at something and still fail; when important relationships are strained; when you have expectations for greatness, but your limitations won't let you achieve them. Many people in the Bible faced discouragement. Elijah was deeply discouraged when he was the last prophet in

Israel and his life was threatened. When you are discouraged, you feel like giving up—on God, friends, family, career, even hope itself. It feels like everyone's against you and nobody cares. What was most important to you now seems trivial. Worst of all, you can't see the way back to joy and happiness. When you reach your lowest point, you must decide whether you will sink deeper into the mire or begin to climb your way up and out of the pit. The opposite of discouragement is encouragement, and it is the antidote you need when you are down. God is your greatest encourager. He never abandons you, and he heals your wounds. He inspires you with his Word; he listens to your prayers and answers them; he revives you with hope. When you feel discouraged, seek God's help first. Then find encouragement from others who can help you put things in perspective. Face head-on the cause of your discouragement, and plan steps to recover. When you see a way out, your hope will return, and over time so will your joy.

DIVINE PROMISE

BE STRONG AND COURAGEOUS! DO NOT
BE AFRAID OR DISCOURAGED. FOR THE
LORD YOUR GOD IS WITH YOU WHEREVER
YOU GO. *Joshua 1:9*

Doubt

MY QUESTION *for* GOD

When I'm struggling with doubt in my Christian life, does it mean I have less faith?

A MOMENT *with* GOD

He has given us great and precious promises. . . . Make every effort to respond to God's promises.

2 PETER 1:4-5

Abram replied, "O Sovereign LORD, how can I be sure that I will actually possess it?" GENESIS 15:8

John the Baptist . . . sent his disciples to ask Jesus, "Are you the Messiah we've been expecting?"

MATTHEW 11:2-3

Many people in the Bible whom we consider to be pillars of the faith had moments of doubt. This doesn't mean that they had less faith but that their faith was being challenged in new ways. When you have moments of doubt, you are probably in new territory. Allow your doubt to move you closer to God, not farther away from him. Then you will find the strength to trust him, and your faith will grow stronger.

DIVINE PROMISE

JESUS TOLD HIM, "YOU BELIEVE BECAUSE YOU HAVE SEEN ME. BLESSED ARE THOSE WHO BELIEVE WITHOUT SEEING ME." *John 20:29*

Emptiness

MY QUESTIONS *for* GOD

Why does my life seem so empty sometimes? How do I fill the emptiness inside me?

A MOMENT *with* GOD

When an evil spirit leaves a person, it goes into the desert, searching for rest. But when it finds none, it says, "I will return to the person I came from." So it returns and finds that its former home is all swept and in order. Then the spirit finds seven other spirits more evil than itself, and they all enter the person and live there. And so that person is worse off than before.   LUKE 11:24-26

Let them no longer fool themselves by trusting in empty riches, for emptiness will be their only reward.

JOB 15:31

May you experience the love of Christ, though it is too great to understand fully. Then you will be made complete with all the fullness of life and power that comes from God.   EPHESIANS 3:19

Jesus replied, "Anyone who drinks this water will soon become thirsty again. But those who drink the water I give will never be thirsty again. It becomes a fresh, bubbling spring within them, giving them eternal life."   JOHN 4:13-14

The traveler whose gas tank is on empty might become stranded miles from the nearest town. The hiker who empties the last few drops of water from his canteen while still a long way from camp might become dehydrated. The husband whose wife dies young might wonder how he can go on, how he can raise his children by himself, how he can fill his empty heart. When something is empty, either it no longer works or it no longer satisfies. But when *someone* is empty, motivation, meaning, and purpose are lost. There seems to be no reason to go on. Many things can cause you to feel empty—the death of a loved one, the end of a friendship, being ignored or rejected. These feelings of emptiness all have one thing in common: some kind of loss. Loss empties your emotional tank and uses up all your reserves. It leaves you hungry and thirsty, looking for something to fill and satisfy the emptiness. This is the moment Satan's been waiting for. He is always ready to move into an empty heart. He tries to deceive you into thinking that what he offers can satisfy you. But only God can fill the emptiness inside you and satisfy your deepest needs. When your heart is filled with the love, truth, and goodness of God, there is no room for evil to enter. It is only through the presence of God's Spirit within you that meaning, purpose, and satisfaction will be restored. God created you to be truly fulfilled when you fill your soul with him.

DIVINE PROMISE

I PRAY THAT GOD, THE SOURCE OF HOPE, WILL FILL YOU COMPLETELY WITH JOY AND PEACE BECAUSE YOU TRUST IN HIM. THEN YOU WILL OVERFLOW WITH CONFIDENT HOPE THROUGH THE POWER OF THE HOLY SPIRIT. *Romans 15:13*

Encouragement

MY QUESTION *for* GOD

How can I find encouragement when I feel overwhelmed?

A MOMENT *with* GOD

Five of you will chase a hundred, and a hundred of you will chase ten thousand! All your enemies will fall beneath your sword.   LEVITICUS 26:8

Each one of you will put to flight a thousand of the enemy, for the LORD your God fights for you, just as he has promised.   JOSHUA 23:10

*B*e encouraged that the power of God is on your side, regardless of the number of enemies against you. God used the young boy David to overcome the giant Goliath. He used Gideon's three hundred soldiers to defeat the vast armies of Midian. And he used the twelve disciples to establish the whole church. You don't have to be above average for God to do great things through you. Knowing that God works through you despite your limitations is a great encouragement.

We also pray that you will be strengthened with all his glorious power so you will have all the endurance and patience you need. May you be filled with joy, always thanking the Father. He has enabled you to share in the inheritance that belongs to his people, who live in the light. For he has rescued us from the kingdom of darkness and transferred us into the Kingdom of his dear Son, who purchased our freedom and forgave our sins.   COLOSSIANS 1:11-14

*B*e encouraged that you have been rescued from sin's control and Satan's power. God, through the power of his Holy Spirit, has given you everything you need to overcome whatever overwhelms you. When you remember that you are already free from sin's deadly power, the problems of this world will lose their grip on you.

DIVINE PROMISE

I AM CERTAIN THAT GOD, WHO BEGAN THE
GOOD WORK WITHIN YOU, WILL CONTINUE
HIS WORK UNTIL IT IS FINALLY FINISHED.
Philippians 1:6

Endurance

Why should I try to keep going when I feel like giving up?

Let's not get tired of doing what is good. At just the right time we will reap a harvest of blessing if we don't give up.   GALATIANS 6:9

If we endure hardship, we will reign with him. If we deny him, he will deny us.   2 TIMOTHY 2:12

I am certain that God, who began the good work within you, will continue his work until it is finally finished on the day when Christ Jesus returns.

PHILIPPIANS 1:6

Dear friends, you always followed my instructions when I was with you. And now that I am away, it is even more important. Work hard to show the results of your salvation, obeying God with deep reverence and fear. For God is working in you, giving you the desire and the power to do what pleases him.

PHILIPPIANS 2:12-13

*E*ndurance can be compared to running a marathon, a grueling race that covers more than twenty-six miles and seems like it takes a lifetime to finish! The goal in a marathon is to run the race well, to endure the challenges along the way, to finish strong and receive the rewards that come with reaching the finish line. Those who finish near the top get tangible rewards such as trophies and cash, but everyone who finishes earns the greater reward of immense satisfaction from completing such a tough race. Life is like a marathon. Endurance is necessary to complete the journey. And there are tangible rewards for finishing strong—a heritage to pass along, a good reputation that others can follow, a legacy to leave behind. But the greatest reward for finishing life well is the prize of eternal life with God. This reward is given to all who have faith in Jesus Christ and who endure the challenges of the Christian life—persecution, ridicule, and temptation. Just as marathoners must train hard to build up their endurance so they can run the race and finish well, so Christians must train to build up endurance for living a life of faith in Jesus and staying strong to the end. When you have built up your endurance, you will not collapse during the race but will be able to push on toward the goal of becoming more and more like Jesus. Finally you cross the finish line into heaven and receive the eternal rewards God has promised. You can strengthen your endurance by focusing on God's promises for the future instead of the problems of the moment.

DIVINE PROMISE

DEAR BROTHERS AND SISTERS, WHEN TROUBLES COME YOUR WAY, CONSIDER IT AN OPPORTUNITY FOR GREAT JOY. FOR YOU KNOW THAT WHEN YOUR FAITH IS TESTED, YOUR ENDURANCE HAS A CHANCE TO GROW.

James 1:2-3

Enemies

MY QUESTION *for* GOD

What does it mean to love my enemies?

A MOMENT *with* GOD

You have heard the law that says, "Love your neighbor" and hate your enemy. But I say, love your enemies! Pray for those who persecute you!

MATTHEW 5:43-44

All of you should be of one mind. Sympathize with each other. Love each other as brothers and sisters. Be tenderhearted, and keep a humble attitude. Don't repay evil for evil. Don't retaliate with insults when people insult you. Instead, pay them back with a blessing. That is what God has called you to do, and he will bless you for it.

1 PETER 3:8-9

Showing love to your enemies seems completely un-reasonable—unless you realize that you were once an enemy of God until he forgave you. When you love your enemy, you see that person as Jesus does—some-one in need of grace and forgiveness. Getting to that point takes prayer. When you pray for others, you can't help but feel compassion for them. If you respond with prayer and blessing instead of retaliation when some-one hurts you, you will experience a divine moment of God's blessing.

DIVINE·PROMISE

IF YOUR ENEMIES ARE HUNGRY, FEED THEM.
IF THEY ARE THIRSTY, GIVE THEM SOMETHING
TO DRINK. . . . DON'T LET EVIL CONQUER YOU,
BUT CONQUER EVIL BY DOING GOOD.

Romans 12:20-21

Enemies

MY QUESTION *for* GOD

Is it possible to turn an enemy into a friend?

A MOMENT *with* GOD

Meanwhile, Saul was uttering threats with every
breath and was eager to kill the Lord's followers.
So he went to the high priest. He requested letters
addressed to the synagogues in Damascus, asking for
their cooperation in the arrest of any followers of the
Way he found there. He wanted to bring them—both
men and women—back to Jerusalem in chains. As
he was approaching Damascus on this mission, a light
from heaven suddenly shone down around him. He
fell to the ground and heard a voice saying to him,
"Saul! Saul! Why are you persecuting me?" "Who are
you, lord?" Saul asked.   ACTS 9:1-5

I used to believe that I ought to do everything I could
to oppose the very name of Jesus the Nazarene.
Indeed, I did just that in Jerusalem. Authorized by
the leading priests, I caused many believers there to
be sent to prison. And I cast my vote against them

when they were condemned to death. Many times I had them punished in the synagogues to get them to curse Jesus. I was so violently opposed to them that I even chased them down in foreign cities.   ACTS 26:9-11

All they knew was that people were saying, "The one who used to persecute us is now preaching the very faith he tried to destroy!"   GALATIANS 1:23

*E*very day, enemies of God become his followers! It is a mystery why he overwhelms some enemies, like Saul, until they turn to his side, but he seems to leave others alone. But in almost every church around the world, you will find believers who once actively opposed God or his people or his way of living but who were eventually persuaded by God's overwhelming love.

Be careful to live properly among your unbelieving neighbors. Then even if they accuse you of doing wrong, they will see your honorable behavior, and they will give honor to God when he judges the world.   1 PETER 2:12

*T*here is no witness more powerful and effective than having someone who was an enemy become a friend. And you can accomplish that with love, forgiveness, prayer, and kind words.

DIVINE PROMISE

THIS INCLUDES YOU WHO WERE ONCE FAR
AWAY FROM GOD. YOU WERE HIS ENEMIES,
SEPARATED FROM HIM BY YOUR EVIL
THOUGHTS AND ACTIONS. YET NOW HE HAS
RECONCILED YOU TO HIMSELF THROUGH THE
DEATH OF CHRIST IN HIS PHYSICAL BODY. AS A
RESULT, HE HAS BROUGHT YOU INTO HIS OWN
PRESENCE, AND YOU ARE HOLY AND BLAMELESS
AS YOU STAND BEFORE HIM WITHOUT
A SINGLE FAULT.   *Colossians 1:21-22*

Eternal Life

MY QUESTION *for* GOD

How should my hope of eternal life affect the way I live now?

A MOMENT *with* GOD

God has made everything beautiful for its own time.
He has planted eternity in the human heart, but even
so, people cannot see the whole scope of God's work
from beginning to end.   ECCLESIASTES 3:11

What do you benefit if you gain the whole world but
lose your own soul? Is anything worth more than
your soul?   MARK 8:36-37

No eye has seen, no ear has heard, and no mind
has imagined what God has prepared for those who
love him.   1 CORINTHIANS 2:9

*K*ing Solomon wrote in the book of Ecclesiastes that God has planted eternity in the human heart. This means that we innately know there is more than just this life. Something we were made for is still missing. Because we are created in God's image, we have eternal value, and nothing but the eternal God can truly satisfy our longings. He has created us with a restless yearning for the kind of perfect world that can only be found in heaven. He gives us a glimpse of that world through nature, art, and relationships. Someday he will restore earth to the way it was when he first created it, and eternity will be a never-ending exploration of its beauty in a perfect relationship with God. If the rewards of this earthly life were all we had to live for, then a "why bother" attitude might be appropriate. But there are two reasons why this perspective is wrong: First, when you try to obey God, you put yourself in a position to enjoy life the way it is meant to be enjoyed; your relationships are faithful, your life has integrity, and your conscience is clear. Second, this life is not all there is. The Bible is clear that those who trust in Jesus Christ and turn to him for forgiveness receive the promise of eternal life. Your faithfulness in this life may or may not result in material prosperity, but the eternal rewards of heaven will be greater than you could ever imagine.

DIVINE PROMISE

I AM THE RESURRECTION AND THE LIFE.
ANYONE WHO BELIEVES IN ME WILL LIVE,
EVEN AFTER DYING. *John 11:25*

Evil

MY QUESTION *for* GOD

If God is good, why does he allow evil in the world?

A MOMENT *with* GOD

The LORD God placed the man in the Garden of Eden
to tend and watch over it. But the LORD God warned
him, "You may freely eat the fruit of every tree in the
garden—except the tree of the knowledge of good
and evil. If you eat its fruit, you are sure to die."

GENESIS 2:15-17

Everyone has sinned; we all fall short of God's
glorious standard.   ROMANS 3:23

Stay alert! Watch out for your great enemy, the devil.
He prowls around like a roaring lion, looking for
someone to devour. Stand firm against him, and be
strong in your faith.   1 PETER 5:8-9

I went into your sanctuary, O God, and I finally
understood the destiny of the wicked. Truly, you
put them on a slippery path and send them sliding
over the cliff to destruction. In an instant they are
destroyed, completely swept away by terrors. When
you arise, O LORD, you will laugh at their silly ideas
as a person laughs at dreams in the morning.

PSALM 73:17-20

𝒢enuine love requires the freedom to choose. From the beginning, God desired a loving relationship with human beings, so he gave us this freedom. But with ability to make choices comes the possibility of choosing a way other than God's way. When we choose our own way, it always leads to sin because we are all born with a sinful nature. This breaks God's heart. But if he hadn't given us the freedom to choose, he would have created robots, not humans. Evil still exists, and evil people continue to do evil things because they choose to. But you can choose to do what is right. When you do, God is greatly pleased, good prevails, and Satan loses ground. Eventually God will completely destroy the power of evil forever. Until that day, you can overcome evil by choosing to obey God.

DIVINE PROMISE

DON'T LET ANYONE CAPTURE YOU WITH EMPTY PHILOSOPHIES AND HIGH-SOUNDING NONSENSE THAT COME FROM HUMAN THINKING AND FROM THE SPIRITUAL POWERS OF THIS WORLD, RATHER THAN FROM CHRIST.

Colossians 2:8

Evil

MY QUESTION for GOD

Is it dangerous to be around evil people?

A MOMENT *with* GOD

The LORD said to Moses and Aaron, "Get away from
all these people so that I may instantly destroy them!"
But Moses and Aaron fell face down on the ground.
"O God," they pleaded, "you are the God who gives
breath to all creatures. Must you be angry with all the
people when only one man sins?" And the LORD said
to Moses, "Then tell all the people to get away from
the tents of Korah, Dathan, and Abiram." So Moses
got up and rushed over to the tents of Dathan and
Abiram, followed by the elders of Israel. "Quick!"
he told the people. "Get away from the tents of these
wicked men, and don't touch anything that belongs to
them. If you do, you will be destroyed for their sins."

NUMBERS 16:20-26

Ultimately, God will judge all evil at the Last Day.
But there have also been times here on earth when
God's anger against evil is poured out in judgment.
There are times when people who consistently live
an evil lifestyle put themselves in harm's way enough
times that harm does eventually come to them. Moses
warned the Israelites to stay away from Korah, Dathan,
and Abiram because God was getting ready to punish
these men for the evil they had done. If others even got
too close to them, they would be in harm's way. Don't
get too close to evil, or you may be harmed spiritually
or physically. If you are attracted to those who do evil
or hang around such people too often, you are in danger of becoming like them and thus experiencing the

Example   101

judgment that will come their way. It is a divine moment when it suddenly dawns on you just how dangerous your situation is if you are too close to evil.

DIVINE PROMISE
THE PATH OF THE WICKED LEADS TO DESTRUCTION.   *Psalm 1:6*

Example

MY QUESTION *for* GOD

What is the role of parents in their children's spiritual development?

A MOMENT *with* GOD

The LORD is our God, the LORD alone. And you must love the LORD your God with all your heart, all your soul, and all your strength. And you must commit yourselves wholeheartedly to these commands that I am giving you today. Repeat them again and again to your children. Talk about them when you are at home and when you are on the road, when you are going to bed and when you are getting up. Tie them to your hands and wear them on your forehead as reminders. Write them on the doorposts of your house and on your gates.   DEUTERONOMY 6:4-9

𝒜 famous professional athlete once said, "I am not a role model; parents are role models." That sports star, however misguided in his underestimation of his own influence, was right about parents. Colloquial wisdom says that spiritual values and character are caught as much as taught. Parents who drop their children off at Sunday school without going to church themselves are as hypocritical as those who light up a cigarette while telling their children not to smoke. The Bible teaches that parents bear the fundamental responsibility for spiritual education of children, and that spiritual values are most effectively taught when they are integrated into the fabric of daily family life. What would a child watching your life conclude about the importance of a relationship with God? As you strive to be a good example, remember God first thing in the morning, and fall asleep with him on your mind. Remember God as the source of hope when you think you've lost all hope. Remember God with a thankful heart when you have plenty, for you will need him when you have little. Meditate on God and his great love for you. Weave him into the fabric of your life so your children and grand-children will be trained from their earliest days to love God with grateful hearts.

DIVINE CHALLENGE

TAKE A NEW GRIP WITH YOUR TIRED HANDS AND STRENGTHEN YOUR WEAK KNEES. MARK OUT A STRAIGHT PATH FOR YOUR FEET SO THAT THOSE WHO ARE WEAK AND LAME WILL NOT FALL BUT BECOME STRONG. *Hebrews 12:12-13*

Excellence

MY QUESTION *for* GOD

Why is it important to strive for excellence?

A MOMENT *with* GOD

God looked over all he had made, and he saw that it
was very good!   GENESIS 1:31

Do you have the gift of helping others? Do it with all
the strength and energy that God supplies.   1 PETER 4:11

Hezekiah encouraged all the Levites regarding the
skill they displayed as they served the LORD.

2 CHRONICLES 30:22

The LORD has filled Bezalel with the Spirit of God,
giving him great wisdom, ability, and expertise in all
kinds of crafts. He is a master craftsman, expert in
working with gold, silver, and bronze. . . . And the
LORD has given both him and Oholiab . . . the ability
to teach their skills to others.   EXODUS 35:31-34

*E*xcellence is performing beyond expectations—and
it is rare for something or someone to exceed expectations. An excellent car will perform even better
than you thought it would, and it will actually make
driving fun. A medical doctor striving for excellence
might develop a new vaccine that saves people's lives.
God wants us to pursue excellence because doing so
shows we care about doing things right, that we care
about helping people to the best of our ability. Pursuing

excellence helps others experience excellence by giving them a glimpse of God's character and inspiring them to pursue excellence themselves. God initiated excellence in the beauty of his creation, and we are called to perpetuate it. Our lives display excellence when we consistently strive to model ourselves after Jesus Christ, who was perfect, and as we go about the work he has called us to do. We'll never be perfect in this life, but as we work toward that goal, we will model excellence to those around us.

Divine Promise

WORK WILLINGLY AT WHATEVER YOU DO, AS THOUGH YOU WERE WORKING FOR THE LORD RATHER THAN FOR PEOPLE. REMEMBER THAT THE LORD WILL GIVE YOU AN INHERITANCE AS YOUR REWARD, AND THAT THE MASTER YOU ARE SERVING IS CHRIST.   *Colossians 3:23-24*

Excuses

My Question *for* God

What's so wrong about making excuses?

A Moment *with* God

When Joseph's brothers saw him coming, they . . . made plans to kill him. . . . Judah said to his brothers, "What will we gain by killing our brother? His blood would just give us a guilty conscience. Instead of hurting him, let's sell him to those Ishmaelite traders. After all, he is our brother—our own flesh and blood!" And his brothers agreed.   GENESIS 37:18, 26-27

*J*oseph's brothers altered their initial plan of killing Joseph to *merely* selling him into slavery. Rationalization of a "lesser" sin does not change sin from being sin. When you find yourself rationalizing your actions, it's time to pause and truthfully assess your motives, your behavior, and the potential consequences. Rationalizing is trying to convince yourself that wrong is right or that sin isn't so bad. For example, you make the excuse that lying is acceptable if it's just a half-truth. You convince yourself that your choices have no consequences. The ironic part about rationalizing is that we think we are brilliant but we are actually acting foolishly. Be aware of how you might be making excuses for your actions rather than standing up for what is right.

DIVINE PROMISE

BE CAREFUL TO LIVE PROPERLY AMONG YOUR UNBELIEVING NEIGHBORS. THEN EVEN IF THEY ACCUSE YOU OF DOING WRONG, THEY WILL SEE YOUR HONORABLE BEHAVIOR, AND THEY WILL GIVE HONOR TO GOD WHEN HE JUDGES THE WORLD.   *1 Peter 2:12*

Expectations

What does God expect of me?

A MOMENT *with* GOD

All praise to God, the Father of our Lord Jesus
Christ. It is by his great mercy that we have been
born again, because God raised Jesus Christ from the
dead. Now we live with great expectation, and we
have a priceless inheritance—an inheritance that is
kept in heaven for you, pure and undefiled, beyond
the reach of change and decay.   1 PETER 1:3-4

How precious are your thoughts about me, O God.
They cannot be numbered! I can't even count them.

PSALM 139:17-18

An expectation is a strong hope or confidence that
something will occur. Expectations can be clearly
expressed: Your boss, for example, tells you what he
wants done and how he wants you to do it! Expectations
can be assumed: Your wife expects you to call when
you will be late. Expectations can become problematic
if they are not clearly expressed or if they are unrealistic. Expectations that are not expressed can lead to
disappointment. Expectations that are unrealistic can
lead to frustration and resentment. Sometimes it seems
like God places unrealistic expectations on us. How
can we possibly obey all of his commands? How can we
love according to his standards? God understands that

humanly speaking these expectations are impossible; but with his help they become possible. God's greatest expectation is not that we live a perfect life but that we love him with all our heart. When you understand that God doesn't expect us to be perfect but rather applauds us when we sincerely try to follow him, it can be a divine moment because you no longer see him as a strict taskmaster but as a loving encourager.

DIVINE PROMISE

THE LORD IS CLOSE TO ALL WHO CALL ON HIM,
YES, TO ALL WHO CALL ON HIM IN TRUTH.
Psalm 145:18

Failure

MY QUESTION *for* GOD

What is failure in God's eyes?

A MOMENT *with* GOD

What do you benefit if you gain the whole world but lose your own soul? Is anything worth more than your soul?   MATTHEW 16:26

Anyone who listens to my teaching and follows it is wise, like a person who builds a house on solid rock. Though the rain comes in torrents and the floodwaters rise and the winds beat against that house, it won't collapse because it is built on bedrock.

But anyone who hears my teaching and doesn't
obey it is foolish, like a person who builds a house
on sand. When the rains and floods come and the
winds beat against that house, it will collapse with
a mighty crash.   MATTHEW 7:24-27

It's your sins that have cut you off from God. Because
of your sins, he has turned away and will not listen
anymore.   ISAIAH 59:2

𝓘f you were to reach the end of your life having managed a successful business, raised a good family, won all
kinds of community awards, and retired comfortably,
would you say your life was a success? God says that
kind of life would be a failure if you did all those things
apart from him. Failure in God's eyes is not living the
way he created you to live. God instructs you to live
his way for a very good reason—to help you make the
most of life, both now and in eternity. God gave you the
gift of life and created you to have a relationship with
him. Your greatest failure would be to reject that life
and the God who gave it to you. Don't fail by neglecting
or ignoring God. He knows the best way to succeed in
life. You will fail if you go against him and try to live
your own way. You will succeed if you discover what a
relationship with God means for your future.

DIVINE PROMISE

THE LORD DIRECTS THE STEPS OF THE GODLY.
HE DELIGHTS IN EVERY DETAIL OF THEIR

LIVES. THOUGH THEY STUMBLE, THEY WILL
NEVER FALL, FOR THE LORD HOLDS THEM BY
THE HAND.   *Psalm 37:23-24*

Faithfulness

MY QUESTION *for* GOD

Why should I be faithful?

A MOMENT *with* GOD

The members of the council were amazed when they
saw the boldness of Peter and John, for they could see
that they were ordinary men with no special training
in the Scriptures. They also recognized them as men
who had been with Jesus.   ACTS 4:13

David replied to the Philistine, "You come to me with
sword, spear, and javelin, but I come to you in the
name of the LORD of Heaven's Armies— the God of
the armies of Israel, whom you have defied. Today
the LORD will conquer you."   1 SAMUEL 17:45-46

God chooses to accomplish great things through faithful people.

Oh, the joys of those who do not follow the advice
of the wicked, or stand around with sinners, or join
in with mockers. But they delight in the law of the
LORD, meditating on it day and night. They are like
trees planted along the riverbank, bearing fruit each

season. Their leaves never wither, and they prosper in
all they do.   PSALM 1:1-3

𝓕aithfulness determines the quality of your character, which affects the quality of your life. Faithfulness
brings vitality and productivity.

Never let loyalty and kindness leave you! . . . Then
you will find favor with both God and people, and
you will earn a good reputation.   PROVERBS 3:3-4

𝓕aithfulness is an essential characteristic of a good
reputation. Others will know they can trust you.
When you run into problems, sometimes faithfulness
is the key to a positive outcome.

This is a trustworthy saying: If we die with him, we
will also live with him. If we endure hardship, we
will reign with him. If we deny him, he will deny
us. If we are unfaithful, he remains faithful, for he
cannot deny who he is.   2 TIMOTHY 2:11-13

𝓕aithfulness is necessary to maintain love. Despite
our sins, God loves and remains faithful to us. Model
the love of Christ to others by remaining faithful to
them even when they fail you.

If you remain faithful even when facing death, I will
give you the crown of life.   REVELATION 2:10

If we are faithful to the end, trusting God just as firmly as when we first believed, we will share in all that belongs to Christ.   HEBREWS 3:14

When someone else shows faithfulness to us, it strengthens our sense of security. And no one but God can show us the kind of faithfulness that builds our confidence in our eternal security.

DIVINE PROMISE

SURELY YOUR GOODNESS AND UNFAILING LOVE WILL PURSUE ME ALL THE DAYS OF MY LIFE.   *Psalm 23:6*

Fear

MY QUESTION *for* GOD

What does it mean to fear God?

A MOMENT *with* GOD

Doesn't his majesty terrify you? Doesn't your fear of him overwhelm you?   JOB 13:11

Let the whole world fear the LORD, and let everyone stand in awe of him.   PSALM 33:8

Fear of the LORD is the foundation of wisdom.

PROVERBS 9:10

*F*earing God is not the same as being afraid of him. If you are afraid of God, you will stay away from him. But fearing God means being awed by his power and goodness. This draws you closer to him and the blessings he gives. Fear of God is like the respect you have for a beloved teacher, coach, parent, or mentor. Your respect motivates you both to do your best and to avoid doing anything that would offend or hurt that person. You fear God because of his awesome power; you love God for the way he blesses you.

Serve the LORD with reverent fear, and rejoice with trembling.   PSALM 2:11

How joyful are those who fear the LORD—all who follow his ways!   PSALM 128:1

*B*ecause God is so great and mighty, and because he holds the power of life and death in his hands, you should have a healthy, reverent fear of him. When you have a healthy fear of God, you recognize what he could do if he gave you what you deserve. A healthy fear should drive you to God for forgiveness. You can also rejoice that instead of punishment, God gives you mercy and forgiveness. He even desires to have a relationship with you.

DIVINE PROMISE

DON'T BE AFRAID, FOR I AM WITH YOU. DON'T BE DISCOURAGED, FOR I AM YOUR GOD. I WILL STRENGTHEN YOU AND HELP YOU. I WILL HOLD YOU UP WITH MY VICTORIOUS RIGHT HAND.

Isaiah 41:10

Fear

MY QUESTION *for* GOD

I have so many fears and concerns. How do I deal with them?

A MOMENT *with* GOD

Moses pleaded with the LORD, "O LORD, I'm not very good with words. I never have been, and I'm not now, even though you have spoken to me. I get tongue-tied, and my words get tangled." Then the LORD asked Moses, "Who makes a person's mouth? . . . I will be with you as you speak, and I will instruct you in what to say."

EXODUS 4:10-12

I love you, LORD; you are my strength. The LORD is my rock, my fortress, and my savior; my God is my rock, in whom I find protection. He is my shield, the power that saves me, and my place of safety. . . . In your strength I can crush an army; with my God I can scale any wall.

PSALM 18:1-2, 29

There are no limits to what God can do in and through you. With his strength, you have the power to do things you could never do on your own. You can withstand the toughest attacks and take the offensive in overcoming your problems. You can live without fear because you rely on God's strength. Give all of your fears to God, and let God give you his strength.

DIVINE PROMISE

I CAN DO EVERYTHING THROUGH CHRIST,
WHO GIVES ME STRENGTH.   *Philippians 4:13*

Finishing

MY QUESTION *for* GOD

What can inspire me to finish well?

A MOMENT *with* GOD

The years passed, and the LORD had given the people
of Israel rest from all their enemies. Joshua, who was
now very old, called together all the elders, leaders,
judges, and officers of Israel. He said to them, "I am
now a very old man. You have seen everything the
LORD your God has done for you during my lifetime.
The LORD your God has fought for you against your
enemies. I have allotted to you as your homeland all
the land of the nations yet unconquered, as well as
the land of those we have already conquered—from
the Jordan River to the Mediterranean Sea in the
west. This land will be yours, for the LORD your
God will himself drive out all the people living there
now. You will take possession of their land, just as
the LORD your God promised you. So be very careful
to follow everything Moses wrote in the Book of
Instruction. Do not deviate from it, turning either to
the right or to the left. . . . Cling tightly to the LORD
your God as you have done until now."   JOSHUA 23:1-8

*A*s the years take a toll on our bodies, it is painful to realize that we no longer possess the physical abilities or the energy we used to have. As old age settles in, the wrinkles, aches, and pains make us realize that our lives are nearing their final chapter. It's even more painful when we see the rest of the world dismissing the elderly as though their earthly contributions are finished. When Joshua was an old man, he demonstrated that older believers can be a powerful witness to the persistent mercy and faithfulness of God. There are few things as powerful as the testimony of someone who has lived a long life of faithfulness to the Lord and still sees a vibrant vision of an eternal God who keeps his promises. Younger people who hear the life stories of such Christians will be greatly impacted by learning of the faithfulness God has shown them through the decades. If you are younger, find an older believer who can tell you about God's faithfulness in his life. Be prepared to hear some amazing stories! If you are older, commit yourself to finishing well. Demonstrate being faithful to God to the end—your story will become a divine moment in the lives of those who follow you.

DIVINE PROMISE

I AM CERTAIN THAT GOD, WHO BEGAN THE GOOD WORK WITHIN YOU, WILL CONTINUE HIS WORK UNTIL IT IS FINALLY FINISHED ON THE DAY WHEN CHRIST JESUS RETURNS.

Philippians 1:6

Forgiveness

MY QUESTION *for* GOD

I've done some pretty awful things. How can God forgive me?

A MOMENT *with* GOD

You are holy and blameless as you stand before him
without a single fault.   COLOSSIANS 1:22

Though your sins are like scarlet, I will make them
as white as snow. Though they are red like crimson,
I will make them as white as wool.   ISAIAH 1:18

When God forgives you, he looks at you as though you
have never sinned; you become blameless before him.
When God forgives you, he doesn't just sweep your sins
under the carpet; he completely washes them away.

Against you, and you alone, have I sinned; I have done
what is evil in your sight.   PSALM 51:4

If we claim we have no sin, we are only fooling
ourselves and not living in the truth. But if we confess
our sins to him, he is faithful and just to forgive us
our sins and to cleanse us from all wickedness.

1 JOHN 1:8-9

If my people who are called by my name will humble
themselves and pray and seek my face and turn from
their wicked ways, I will hear from heaven and will
forgive their sins and restore their land.

2 CHRONICLES 7:14

*R*ealize that God is the one who has ultimately been wronged by your sin, so you should seek forgiveness from him first. Confessing your sin is the first step in receiving forgiveness. To confess your sin means to agree with God that you have done something wrong. Because Jesus Christ died to take the punishment for your sin and rose from the dead to show his power over death, God accepts your confession and forgives you. There is nothing more you must do. Don't allow lingering feelings of shame to persuade you otherwise.

This is my blood, which confirms the covenant between God and his people. It is poured out as a sacrifice to forgive the sins of many.   MATTHEW 26:28

*J*esus died on the cross so that God's forgiveness would be freely available to you. Jesus took the punishment you deserve. He paid your debt in full. All you need to do is accept God's gift of forgiveness.

The sacrifice you desire is a broken spirit. You will not reject a broken and repentant heart, O God.

PSALM 51:17

*G*od is more ready to forgive than you may be to repent. A broken and humble heart is the quickest way to spiritual wholeness.

I tell you the truth, all sin and blasphemy can be forgiven.   MARK 3:28

Everyone who calls on the name of the LORD will
be saved.   JOEL 2:32

Nothing can ever separate us from God's love.

                                                ROMANS 8:38

He forgives all my sins and heals all my diseases.
. . . He does not punish us for all our sins; he does
not deal harshly with us, as we deserve. For his
unfailing love toward those who fear him is as great
as the height of the heavens above the earth. He has
removed our sins as far from us as the east is from
the west.   PSALM 103:3, 10-12

*F*orgiveness is not based on the magnitude of the sin
but on the magnitude of the forgiver's love. Nothing
you've done is so bad that God's complete and unconditional love can't forgive it. However, the Bible does
mention one unforgivable sin: harboring an attitude of
defiant hostility toward God that prevents you from
accepting his forgiveness (see Mark 3:29 and Matthew
12:31). Only those who don't want God's forgiveness
are out of its reach.

DIVINE PROMISE

"MY WAYWARD CHILDREN," SAYS THE LORD,
"COME BACK TO ME, AND I WILL HEAL YOUR
WAYWARD HEARTS." *Jeremiah 3:22*

Future

MY QUESTION *for* GOD

Why doesn't God show me more of the future?

A MOMENT *with* GOD

That is what the Scriptures mean when they say,
"No eye has seen, no ear has heard, and no mind has
imagined what God has prepared for those who love
him."   1 CORINTHIANS 2:9

The LORD of Heaven's Armies has sworn this oath:
"It will all happen as I have planned. It will be as I
have decided."   ISAIAH 14:24

*G*od reveals enough of the future to give you hope. He
tells you that there is a heaven, he tells you how to get
to heaven, and he tells you that your future in heaven
will be more wonderful than you can imagine. Perhaps
knowing more details than that would be too much for
anyone to take in.

The LORD had said to Abram, "Leave your native
country, your relatives, and your father's family, and
go to the land that I will show you. I will make you
into a great nation. I will bless you and make you
famous, and you will be a blessing to others." . . .
So Abram departed as the LORD had instructed.

                                                GENESIS 12:1-4

Jesus replied, "If I want him to remain alive until I
return, what is that to you? As for you, follow me."

                                                JOHN 21:22

God reveals enough of the future to encourage you to obey. To receive God's rewards in the future requires your obedience in the present.

Look here, you who say, "Today or tomorrow we are going to a certain town and will stay there a year. We will do business there and make a profit." How do you know what your life will be like tomorrow? Your life is like the morning fog—it's here a little while, then it's gone. What you ought to say is, "If the Lord wants us to, we will live and do this or that." Otherwise you are boasting about your own plans, and all such boasting is evil.   JAMES 4:13-16

Humble yourselves before the Lord, and he will lift you up in honor.   JAMES 4:10

God reveals enough of the future to increase your dependence on him. God alone knows everything about the future, and he wants you to be a part of his work in it, so you must rely on him to lead you there. That is the essence of what it means to live by faith. Faith is trusting God to lead you into the future he promises you rather than trying to create your own future by yourself.

DIVINE PROMISE

YOU GUIDE ME WITH YOUR COUNSEL, LEADING ME TO A GLORIOUS DESTINY.   *Psalm 73:24*

Gentleness

MY QUESTIONS *for* GOD

What does gentleness accomplish? Won't people walk all over me if I am gentle?

A MOMENT *with* GOD

The Holy Spirit produces this kind of fruit in our lives: love, joy, peace, patience, kindness, goodness, faithfulness, gentleness, and self-control. There is no law against these things!   GALATIANS 5:22-23

You should clothe yourselves instead with the beauty that comes from within, the unfading beauty of a gentle and quiet spirit, which is so precious to God.

1 PETER 3:4

Pursue righteousness and a godly life, along with faith, love, perseverance, and gentleness. 1 TIMOTHY 6:11

*B*eing gentle does not mean you should be anyone's doormat. God is the perfect example of gentleness, yet he is also a mighty warrior who defeats the powers of hell. In God's eyes, gentle people are the most powerful and influential in the world because they make an impact on others without the use of force or conflict. Gentleness may be your most powerful weapon of influence because you can accomplish much more by gentleness than by coercion.

DIVINE PROMISE

GOD BLESSES THOSE WHO ARE HUMBLE, FOR THEY WILL INHERIT THE WHOLE EARTH.

Matthew 5:5

Generosity

MY QUESTION *for* GOD

What would generosity look like in my life?

A MOMENT *with* GOD

While Jesus was in the Temple, he watched the rich people dropping their gifts in the collection box. Then a poor widow came by and dropped in two small coins. "I tell you the truth," Jesus said, "this poor widow has given more than all the rest of them. For they have given a tiny part of their surplus, but she, poor as she is, has given everything she has."

LUKE 21:1-4

[Jesus said,] "Wherever your treasure is, there the desires of your heart will also be."   MATTHEW 6:21

Don't forget to do good and to share with those in need. These are the sacrifices that please God.

HEBREWS 13:16

You must each decide in your heart how much to give. And don't give reluctantly or in response to pressure. "For God loves a person who gives cheerfully."

2 CORINTHIANS 9:7

𝒲ho is more generous—a billionaire who gives one million dollars to his church or a poor single mom who gives a hundred? But if you do have a lot of money, does that mean you are not generous? Jesus said you can't know the answer to these questions without knowing the heart of the giver. One thing is clear: Whatever you spend your money on reveals what you care about most. God doesn't focus on how much money you have but on how generous you are with it. It's not what you have but what you do with what you have that's significant—whether it's money, time, or talents. Generosity is both a spiritual gift and a spiritual discipline. Generosity comes easy to some people; others must work hard at it. But no one can afford to neglect it. Generosity is an important character trait in God's eyes because it is the opposite of selfishness. Selfishness promotes greed, stinginess, envy, and hard-heartedness—all traits that destroy relationships. Generosity promotes giving, trust, mercy, and putting the needs of others above your own—all traits that build relationships. And true generosity involves sacrifice, which is the key to changing stinginess into selflessness. When you realize that everything you have is a gift from our generous God, you will be motivated to share your material resources and earthly possessions more freely.

DIVINE PROMISE

REMEMBER THE WORDS OF THE LORD JESUS: "IT IS MORE BLESSED TO GIVE THAN TO RECEIVE."

Acts 20:35

Goals

MY QUESTION *for* GOD

What is one of the most important goals I should have?

A MOMENT *with* GOD

Create in me a clean heart, O God. Renew a loyal spirit within me.   PSALM 51:10

Do not despise these small beginnings, for the LORD rejoices to see the work begin.   ZECHARIAH 4:10

Let the Spirit renew your thoughts and attitudes. Put on your new nature.   EPHESIANS 4:23-24

*Y*ou harvest what you plant: Pumpkin seeds produce pumpkins, sunflower seeds produce sunflowers. That is why you should ask the Lord to plant within you a good heart so that your life will produce good thoughts, motives, and actions. If any bad desires or thoughts remain, it is evidence that some bad seeds have also been planted, and you need to do some weeding. Complete renewal is not yet accomplished because none of us can be entirely pure in this life. But developing purity of mind and heart is one of the worthiest goals you can pursue. Is it one of your goals? More than anything else, a clean heart and mind will impact your relationship with God, your family, and your friends. How might you be different a year from now—inside and outside—if you accomplished this goal?

DIVINE PROMISE

LET'S NOT GET TIRED OF DOING WHAT IS
GOOD. AT JUST THE RIGHT TIME WE WILL REAP
A HARVEST OF BLESSING IF WE DON'T GIVE UP.

Galatians 6:9

Greatness

MY QUESTION *for* GOD

What is greatness in God's eyes?

A MOMENT *with* GOD

Let's build a great city for ourselves with a tower that
reaches into the sky. This will make us famous.

GENESIS 11:4

Jesus said to his disciples, "If any of you wants to be
my follower, you must turn from your selfish ways,
take up your cross, and follow me."   MATTHEW 16:24

When children play "pretend" they almost always pretend to be someone great—a heroic firefighter, a brave
soldier, a brilliant astronaut, a caring schoolteacher.
Such games are innocent enough and might in fact
inspire them to greatness. This kind of pretending is
healthy, but somewhere between childhood and adult-
hood the innocence of pretending is lost. It often turns
into an unhealthy way of hiding the parts of us we are
ashamed of. We pose as someone greater than who we
really are. God warns against pretending to be something we're not, especially if we're pretending to be

spiritually great. There's a difference between wanting
to be a part of God's great work and wanting to achieve
personal greatness through doing God's work. If you're
not sure which side you're on, examine your motives.
If the greatest benefactor of your achievements is yourself, then perhaps you are trying to find greatness in the
wrong way. True greatness comes from knowing your
real value in God's eyes and being honest with yourself
and others. It is better to be honest about your failures
than to lie about your successes. That is why humility
is necessary for true greatness. Don't be fooled into
striving to gain everything you desire in this world at
the cost of your eternal rewards in heaven.

DIVINE CHALLENGE

WHOEVER WANTS TO BE FIRST MUST TAKE LAST
PLACE AND BE THE SERVANT OF EVERYONE ELSE.
Mark 9:35

Grief

MY QUESTION *for* GOD

*How should I respond to sin in my own life, in my church,
and in the world?*

A MOMENT *with* GOD

While Ezra prayed and made this confession, weeping
and lying face down on the ground in front of the
Temple of God, a very large crowd of people from

Israel—men, women, and children—gathered and wept bitterly with him.   EZRA 10:1

Come close to God, and God will come close to you. Wash your hands, you sinners; purify your hearts, for your loyalty is divided between God and the world. Let there be tears for what you have done. Let there be sorrow and deep grief. Let there be sadness instead of laughter, and gloom instead of joy. Humble yourselves before the Lord, and he will lift you up in honor.   JAMES 4:8-10

The kind of sorrow God wants us to experience leads us away from sin and results in salvation. There's no regret for that kind of sorrow. But worldly sorrow, which lacks repentance, results in spiritual death.

                    2 CORINTHIANS 7:10

Grief is an appropriate response to sin. When you grieve, you mourn for something you have lost. Sin causes you to lose much: your intimate relationship with God, the knowledge of the Lord's plan for your life, the Holy Spirit's empowerment to live the Christian life, wholeness within yourself and in your relationships with others, and the ability to be a pure and effective witness to others. What a huge loss! The sorrow you feel over your sin should lead you to a divine moment when you ask God for forgiveness and commit to changing your behavior.

THE LORD IS CLOSE TO THE BROKENHEARTED;
HE RESCUES THOSE WHOSE SPIRITS
ARE CRUSHED.   *Psalm 34:18*

Guarding Your Heart

MY QUESTIONS *for* GOD

What does it mean to guard my heart? Why is it important?

A MOMENT *with* GOD

Guard your heart above all else, for it determines the
course of your life.   PROVERBS 4:23

I say, anyone who even looks at a woman with lust has
already committed adultery with her in his heart.

MATTHEW 5:28

It is what comes from inside that defiles you. For
from within, out of a person's heart, come evil
thoughts, sexual immorality, . . . lustful desires.

MARK 7:20-22

Your eye is a lamp that provides light for your body.
When your eye is good, your whole body is filled
with light.   LUKE 11:34

Ultimately your actions come from your heart.
What you do shows the condition of your heart. Left

unchecked, wrong desires and thoughts will eventually result in wrong actions. For example, if you allow yourself to think about having sex with someone who is not your spouse, your heart will begin to convince you that it's okay. The Bible says that "the human heart is the most deceitful of all things, and desperately wicked" (Jeremiah 17:9). In other words, don't trust your emotions to tell you the difference between right and wrong. Trust God's Word; it comes from God's heart, which is good and perfect.

Divine Promise

PRAY ABOUT EVERYTHING. TELL GOD WHAT YOU NEED, AND THANK HIM FOR ALL HE HAS DONE. THEN YOU WILL EXPERIENCE GOD'S PEACE, WHICH EXCEEDS ANYTHING WE CAN UNDERSTAND. HIS PEACE WILL GUARD YOUR HEARTS AND MINDS AS YOU LIVE IN CHRIST JESUS. *Philippians 4:6-7*

Habits

My Question *for* God

Why should I make a habit of reading the Bible?

A Moment *with* God

When he sits on the throne as king, he must copy for himself this body of instruction on a scroll in the presence of the Levitical priests. He must always

keep that copy with him and read it daily as long as
he lives. That way he will learn to fear the LORD his
God by obeying all the terms of these instructions
and decrees. This regular reading will prevent him
from becoming proud and acting as if he is above his
fellow citizens. It will also prevent him from turning
away from these commands in the smallest way. And
it will ensure that he and his descendants will reign
for many generations in Israel.   DEUTERONOMY 17:18-20

Jesus told him, "No! The Scriptures say, 'People do
not live by bread alone, but by every word that comes
from the mouth of God.'"   MATTHEW 4:4

Imagine asking, "Should I eat regularly, or just once
every few days?" Ridiculous! You need to eat regularly
every day because you need food to live. Jesus taught
that God's Word is spiritual food that you need to
depend on for spiritual life. The Bible provides daily
nourishment for your soul. This means you can't just
read the Bible whenever you get around to it. It is only
through regular Bible study that you can maintain the
right perspective on sin, holiness, and God's love. If
you do not make a habit of reading the Bible, you will
inevitably drift away from God. If you are apart from
God, you will have no chance to experience the mercy
and blessings that come from a relationship with him.

DIVINE PROMISE

EVEN MORE BLESSED ARE ALL WHO HEAR THE WORD OF GOD AND PUT IT INTO PRACTICE.

Luke 11:28

Hand of God

MY QUESTIONS *for* GOD

Does God really work in my life? How can I be aware of what he is doing?

A MOMENT *with* GOD

Who can list the glorious miracles of the LORD? Who can ever praise him enough?   PSALM 106:2

Now I said to them, "You know very well what trouble we are in. Jerusalem lies in ruins, and its gates have been destroyed by fire. Let us rebuild the wall of Jerusalem and end this disgrace!" Then I told them about how the gracious hand of God had been on me, and about my conversation with the king. They replied at once, "Yes, let's rebuild the wall!" So they began the good work.   NEHEMIAH 2:17-18

"Yes," says the LORD, "I will do mighty miracles for you, like those I did when I rescued you from slavery in Egypt."   MICAH 7:15

Maybe you think that God's work on this earth comes only in the form of dramatic miracles, like raising someone from the dead. But all around you are supernatural occurrences from the hand of God. They may not be as dramatic as the parting of the Red Sea, but they are no less powerful. Think of the birth of a baby, the healing of an illness, the rebirth of the earth in spring, the restoration of broken relationships through the work of love and forgiveness, the salvation of sinners through faith alone, the specific call of God in your life. These are just a few ways God acts in his creation. If you think you've never seen the hand of God at work, look closer. He is active all around you.

DIVINE PROMISE

SEEK HIS WILL IN ALL YOU DO, AND HE WILL SHOW YOU WHICH PATH TO TAKE.   *Proverbs 3:6*

Hard-Heartedness

MY QUESTION *for* GOD

What are the signs of a hard heart?

A MOMENT *with* GOD

Pharaoh's heart, however, remained hard. He still refused to listen, just as the LORD had predicted.

EXODUS 7:13

The older brother was angry and wouldn't go in. His father came out and begged him, but he replied, "All these years I've slaved for you and never once refused to do a single thing you told me to. And in all that time you never gave me even one young goat for a feast with my friends. Yet when this son of yours comes back after squandering your money on prostitutes, you celebrate by killing the fattened calf!" His father said to him, "Look, dear son, you have always stayed by me, and everything I have is yours. We had to celebrate this happy day. For your brother was dead and has come back to life! He was lost, but now he is found!"   Luke 15:28-32

"Oh no, sir!" [Hannah] replied. "I haven't been drinking wine or anything stronger. But I am very discouraged, and I was pouring out my heart to the Lord.   1 Samuel 1:15

Pharaoh had a hard, stubborn heart. No matter how much he heard about God, no matter how many miracles he saw, he still refused to believe. The older brother of the Prodigal Son also struggled with a hard heart. He was more eager to punish than to forgive. Hannah, however, continued to pray to God even when nothing seemed to happen. You must constantly evaluate the condition of your heart. Is it becoming more and more hard and stubborn or open and pliable? Are you reaching out to God despite your circumstances? If you find it hard to forgive others or if you struggle to see God at work in your daily life, then your heart may be hardening. If you don't change course, you will cut yourself off from God, the only One who can really help you. A hard heart rejects God's love, which is the

only thing that can save it. A heart that is right with
God will seek his help and acknowledge his perfectly
timed responses.

DIVINE PROMISE

I WILL GIVE YOU A NEW HEART, AND I WILL
PUT A NEW SPIRIT IN YOU. I WILL TAKE OUT
YOUR STONY, STUBBORN HEART AND GIVE YOU
A TENDER, RESPONSIVE HEART.   *Ezekiel 36:26*

Heart

MY QUESTION *for* GOD

How can my heart become the kind of heart God wants?

A MOMENT *with* GOD

I will give you a new heart, and I will put a new spirit
in you. I will take out your stony, stubborn heart and
give you a tender, responsive heart.   EZEKIEL 36:26

You must first desire a change of heart. Then God
will give it to you!

When the LORD saw their change of heart, he gave
this message to Shemaiah: "Since the people have
humbled themselves, I will not completely destroy
them and will soon give them some relief."

2 CHRONICLES 12:7

*D*evelop an attitude of humility. When you are humble, you show that you are open to God's work in your life.

Put all your rebellion behind you, and find yourselves a new heart and a new spirit.   EZEKIEL 18:31

*G*et rid of any sinful habit or lifestyle. Practice obeying God's Word, and you will see your heart change for the better.

Just think how much more the blood of Christ will purify our consciences from sinful deeds so that we can worship the living God. For by the power of the eternal Spirit, Christ offered himself to God as a perfect sacrifice for our sins.   HEBREWS 9:14

*B*elieve that Jesus died for your sins. He forgives you and purifies your heart.

Create in me a clean heart, O God. Renew a loyal spirit within me.   PSALM 51:10

Let the Spirit renew your thoughts and attitudes. Put on your new nature.   EPHESIANS 4:23-24

A clean heart produces clean thoughts and actions. Don't allow sin to take root and produce bad thoughts and actions.

DIVINE PROMISE

CHRIST WILL MAKE HIS HOME IN YOUR
HEARTS AS YOU TRUST IN HIM. YOUR ROOTS
WILL GROW DOWN INTO GOD'S LOVE AND
KEEP YOU STRONG.   *Ephesians 3:17*

Help

MY QUESTION *for* GOD

How can I overcome my reluctance to ask for help?

A MOMENT *with* GOD

Whenever they were in trouble and turned to the
LORD, the God of Israel, and sought him out, they
found him.   2 CHRONICLES 15:4

The LORD God said, "It is not good for the man to be
alone. I will make a helper who is just right for him."

GENESIS 2:18

If someone has enough money to live well and sees a
brother or sister in need but shows no compassion—
how can God's love be in that person?   1 JOHN 3:17

Two people are better off than one, for they can help
each other succeed. If one person falls, the other can
reach out and help. But someone who falls alone is in
real trouble.   ECCLESIASTES 4:9-10

$\mathscr{A}$ll of us have limitations. We have areas of weakness, we experience feelings of inadequacy, or we lack a particular skill or ability. Sometimes we just don't know what to do or how to do it. Sometimes a crisis strikes, and we can't handle it by ourselves. We need help. It goes against our cultural admiration of the strong, independent spirit, but the truth is that no one can really survive alone. That's why God created us to be in relationship with other people. That means giving and receiving help. We need help to get work done. We need help to restore a relationship. We need help to develop our skills. We need help thinking through a problem. We need help to say "I'm sorry." God wants to help you, too. He is your ultimate helper, for he is wiser, stronger, and more loving than any person you know. Cultivate the habit of seeking help from God and from others, and offer help to those in need. You will experience a divine moment when God comes to your rescue, or you may pass along a divine moment to others when they see God helping them through you.

DIVINE PROMISE

THE LORD IS MY STRENGTH AND SHIELD. I TRUST HIM WITH ALL MY HEART. HE HELPS ME, AND MY HEART IS FILLED WITH JOY.   *Psalm 28:7*

Holiness

MY QUESTION *for* GOD

What does it mean to be holy and to live a holy life?

A MOMENT *with* GOD

I am writing . . . to you who have been called by
God to be his own holy people. He made you holy
by means of Christ Jesus, just as he did for all people
everywhere who call on the name of our Lord Jesus
Christ, their Lord and ours.

1 CORINTHIANS 1:2

You were cleansed; you were made holy.

1 CORINTHIANS 6:11

I plead with you to give your bodies to God because
of all he has done for you. Let them be a living and
holy sacrifice—the kind he will find acceptable.

ROMANS 12:1

Think of holiness as both a journey and a final destination. To be completely holy is to be sinless, pure,
and perfect before God. Of course, no one is perfect,
but that is our ultimate goal. We will reach that final
destination when we stand before God in heaven. But
holiness also means to be different, to be set apart by
God for a specific purpose. We are to be different from
the rest of the world. Our lives are to be a journey toward holiness so that we become a little more pure and
sinless with each passing day. If you strive to be holy on

your earthly journey, you will one day arrive at your
final destination and stand holy before God.

DIVINE PROMISE

EVEN BEFORE HE MADE THE WORLD, GOD
LOVED US AND CHOSE US IN CHRIST TO BE
HOLY AND WITHOUT FAULT IN HIS EYES.

Ephesians 1:4

Holy Spirit

MY QUESTION *for* GOD

How does the Holy Spirit help me?

A MOMENT *with* GOD

I pray that from his glorious, unlimited resources
he will empower you with inner strength through
his Spirit.   EPHESIANS 3:16

You will receive power when the Holy Spirit comes
upon you. And you will be my witnesses, telling
people about me everywhere.   ACTS 1:8

We have received God's Spirit (not the world's spirit),
so we can know the wonderful things God has freely
given us.   1 CORINTHIANS 2:12

Let the Holy Spirit guide your lives. Then you won't
be doing what your sinful nature craves. The sinful
nature wants to do evil, which is just the opposite of

what the Spirit wants. And the Spirit gives us desires
that are the opposite of what the sinful nature desires.

GALATIANS 5:16-17

*T*he Holy Spirit is the power of God, and he lives
in every believer. When you give control of your life
to the Lord, the Holy Spirit releases his power within
you—power to resist temptation, to serve and love
God and others, to endure when you are at the end of
your rope, to have wisdom in all circumstances, and
to persevere in living for God here on earth with the
promise of eternal life in heaven. Through his Spirit,
God gives you the energy and the resources you need
to do whatever he asks you to do.

DIVINE PROMISE

THE HOLY SPIRIT PRODUCES THIS KIND
OF FRUIT IN OUR LIVES: LOVE, JOY,
PEACE, PATIENCE, KINDNESS, GOODNESS,
FAITHFULNESS, GENTLENESS, AND
SELF-CONTROL.   *Galatians 5:22-23*

Hope

MY QUESTION *for* GOD

What am I supposed to be hoping for?

A Moment *with* God

All praise to God, the Father of our Lord Jesus
Christ. It is by his great mercy that we have been
born again, because God raised Jesus Christ from the
dead. Now we live with great expectation, and we
have a priceless inheritance—an inheritance that is
kept in heaven for you, pure and undefiled, beyond
the reach of change and decay. And through your
faith, God is protecting you by his power until you
receive this salvation, which is ready to be revealed
on the last day for all to see. So be truly glad. There is
wonderful joy ahead, even though you have to endure
many trials for a little while.   1 Peter 1:3-6

"I know the plans I have for you," says the Lord.
"They are plans for good and not for disaster, to give
you a future and a hope."   Jeremiah 29:11

For a prisoner on death row, a pardon offers hope of
freedom. We were once spiritual prisoners facing eternal death because of our sin, but God gave us ultimate
hope by forgiving our sins so we can be with him forever in heaven. When life seems impossible, God gives
eternal hope. Hope is essential for persevering through
the tough times. Without hope, we would give up. Just
as focusing on a fixed point in the distance helps you
move in a straighter line, Jesus' followers should fix
their eyes on the eternal horizon. Heaven is where you
will live with God forever, with no pain or sorrow or
suffering. As you move straight toward your goal, the

hope you have for eternity will help you endure the discomforts and trials of daily life.

DIVINE PROMISE

O LORD, YOU ALONE ARE MY HOPE.   *Psalm 71:5*

Humility

MY QUESTION *for* GOD

What is true humility?

A MOMENT *with* GOD

Anyone who becomes as humble as this little child is the greatest in the Kingdom of Heaven.   MATTHEW 18:4

Don't be selfish; don't try to impress others. Be humble, thinking of others as better than yourselves. . . . You must have the same attitude that Christ Jesus had. Though he was God, he did not think of equality with God as something to cling to. Instead, he gave up his divine privileges; he took the humble position of a slave and was born as a human being. When he appeared in human form, he humbled himself in obedience to God and died a criminal's death on a cross.   PHILIPPIANS 2:3-8

Humility is the honest recognition of your own worth—your worth as God sees you. It is the delicate balance between recognizing your sin and knowing how much God loves and values you. Pride is wrong because it elevates you above others, and often above God himself. But degrading yourself is also unaccept-able because it denies the value God placed upon you. He created you in his image and sent his Son to die for you. Jesus did not die for worms but for people he loves very much. Therefore, we have great value in God's eyes. To see yourself as God sees you is true humility. And true humility is the pathway to discovering how to serve God and other people.

DIVINE PROMISE

PRIDE LEADS TO DISGRACE, BUT WITH HUMILITY COMES WISDOM. *Proverbs 11:2*

Imagination

MY QUESTION *for* GOD

How can I use my imagination in my walk with God?

A MOMENT *with* GOD

In that day the wolf and the lamb will live together; the leopard will lie down with the baby goat. The calf and the yearling will be safe with the lion, and a little child will lead them all. The cow will graze near the bear. The cub and the calf will lie down together. The lion will eat hay like a cow. The baby will play safely near the hole of a cobra. Yes, a little child will

put its hand in a nest of deadly snakes without harm.
Nothing will hurt or destroy in all my holy mountain,
for as the waters fill the sea, so the earth will be filled
with people who know the LORD.   ISAIAH 11:6-9

In Jerusalem, the LORD of Heaven's Armies will
spread a wonderful feast for all the people of the
world. It will be a delicious banquet with clear,
well-aged wine and choice meat.   ISAIAH 25:6

Look! I am creating new heavens and a new earth, and
no one will even think about the old ones anymore.

ISAIAH 65:17

I heard a loud shout from the throne, saying, "Look,
God's home is now among his people! He will live
with them, and they will be his people. God himself
will be with them. He will wipe every tear from their
eyes, and there will be no more death or sorrow or
crying or pain. All these things are gone forever."

REVELATION 21:3-4

Imagine a perfect world, where everyone loves each
other and lives together in peace. Picture a place where
there is no crime, no death, no disease, no disappointment or hurt. Even animals have no fear of each other.
Imagine a banquet that lasts forever. You have just pic-
tured heaven and eternal life with God. You can use
your imagination to help you see how wonderful eternity will be. This should motivate you today to live a
life that is pleasing to God and to share your faith with
as many people as you can.

DIVINE PROMISE

THAT IS WHAT THE SCRIPTURES MEAN
WHEN THEY SAY, "NO EYE HAS SEEN, NO EAR
HAS HEARD, AND NO MIND HAS IMAGINED
WHAT GOD HAS PREPARED FOR THOSE WHO
LOVE HIM."   *1 Corinthians 2:9*

Impact

MY QUESTION *for* GOD

*As a Christian, how can I have the greatest impact on
my community?*

A MOMENT *with* GOD

Owe nothing to anyone—except for your obligation
to love one another.   ROMANS 13:8

You must worship Christ as Lord of your life. And
if someone asks about your Christian hope, always
be ready to explain it. But do this in a gentle and
respectful way. Keep your conscience clear. Then if
people speak against you, they will be ashamed when·
they see what a good life you live because you belong
to Christ.   1 PETER 3:15-16

God's influence in the lives of Christians often attracts
others. The more you reflect God's perfect character
traits, the more people will be drawn to you and want
to be around you. Although we all make plenty of mistakes, your goal should be to live in a way that people

around you say, "We can plainly see that God is with you." Would people in your community be able to say that about you? When they do, it's a divine moment for them and for you.

DIVINE PROMISE

YOU ARE THE LIGHT OF THE WORLD. . . . NO ONE LIGHTS A LAMP AND THEN PUTS IT UNDER A BASKET. INSTEAD, A LAMP IS PLACED ON A STAND, WHERE IT GIVES LIGHT TO EVERYONE IN THE HOUSE. IN THE SAME WAY, LET YOUR GOOD DEEDS SHINE OUT FOR ALL TO SEE, SO THAT EVERYONE WILL PRAISE YOUR HEAVENLY FATHER.   *Matthew 5:14-16*

Impossible

MY QUESTION *for* GOD

Can God do the impossible for me?

A MOMENT *with* GOD

He rescues and saves his people; he performs miraculous signs and wonders in the heavens and on earth. He has rescued Daniel from the power of the lions.   DANIEL 6:27

Those who heard this said, "Then who in the world can be saved?" He replied, "What is impossible for people is possible with God."   LUKE 18:26-27

The Lord kept his word and did for Sarah exactly what he had promised. She became pregnant, and she gave birth to a son for Abraham in his old age. This happened at just the time God had said it would.

GENESIS 21:1-2

This is what the Lord of Heaven's Armies says:
All this may seem impossible to you now, a small remnant of God's people. But is it impossible for me? says the Lord of Heaven's Armies.   ZECHARIAH 8:6

The Bible is filled with stories of the impossible: A flood covers the earth, a sea is parted so people can walk through, the sun keeps shining until a battle can be won, a man survives three days in the belly of a fish, a virgin gives birth to a baby boy. To the person who does not believe in God or the authority of the Bible, these stories defy logic. But those who believe in the Creator of all things also believe that he can alter what he has created; he can break natural law to cause something supernatural. In order to experience the impossible and recognize it for what it is, you need faith. Faith opens up a new dimension so you can understand that what you see with your eyes is not all there is. You can recognize the "impossible" things God does for his people because you believe that anything is possible for him. Learn to recognize and appreciate the impossible things God accomplishes for you and around you each day: the gift of forgiveness, the change of seasons, the intricacies of the human body and its ability to heal, the exact conditions needed to support life on this earth, the birth of a baby.

The more you see the impossible acts of God with eyes of faith, the stronger your faith in God will become. There should be no doubt that God specializes in doing what from a human perspective is impossible. But the end of your abilities is the beginning of his. The God who spoke all creation into being can do the impossible for you. Simply believe that he can—and that he wants to.

DIVINE PROMISE

NOW ALL GLORY TO GOD, WHO IS ABLE, THROUGH HIS MIGHTY POWER AT WORK WITHIN US, TO ACCOMPLISH INFINITELY MORE THAN WE MIGHT ASK OR THINK.   *Ephesians 3:20*

Integrity

MY QUESTION *for* GOD

How do I become a man of integrity?

A MOMENT *with* GOD

No, O people, the LORD has told you what is good, and this is what he requires of you: to do what is right, to love mercy, and to walk humbly with your God.   MICAH 6:8

The LORD asked Satan, "Have you noticed my servant Job? He is the finest man in all the earth. He is blameless—a man of complete integrity. He fears God and stays away from evil. And he has maintained his integrity, even though you urged me to harm him without cause."   JOB 2:3

Who may worship in your sanctuary, LORD? Who may enter your presence on your holy hill? Those who lead blameless lives and do what is right, speaking the truth from sincere hearts. Those who refuse to gossip or harm their neighbors or speak evil of their friends. Those who despise flagrant sinners, and honor the faithful followers of the LORD, and keep their promises even when it hurts. Those who lend money without charging interest, and who cannot be bribed to lie about the innocent. Such people will stand firm forever.   PSALM 15:1-5

Integrity is essentially how well your character corresponds to the character of God. Your goal should be to reflect the heart, mind, and actions of Jesus. Integrity allows you to enjoy fellowship with God and helps you live under his protection and guidance. When you lack integrity, you are more vulnerable to sin and negative consequences, especially the disintegration of your character. Developing integrity is a process. Just as gold is made pure through a refining process that tests the metal with fire, so you are made pure through the refining process of gaining integrity. God uses the everyday trials and circumstances of your life to test you and see how pure you are. If the Lord finds that your heart and actions are becoming increasingly pure through this testing, then your character is becoming more like his, and you are gradually gaining integrity.

DIVINE PROMISE

BE CAREFUL TO LIVE PROPERLY AMONG YOUR
UNBELIEVING NEIGHBORS. THEN EVEN IF THEY
ACCUSE YOU OF DOING WRONG, THEY WILL
SEE YOUR HONORABLE BEHAVIOR, AND THEY
WILL GIVE HONOR TO GOD WHEN HE JUDGES
THE WORLD.   *1 Peter 2:12*

Intimacy

MY QUESTION *for* GOD

How do I develop intimacy with God?

A MOMENT *with* GOD

"When that day comes," says the LORD, "you will call
me 'my husband' instead of 'my master.' . . . I will
make you my wife forever, showing you righteousness
and justice, unfailing love and compassion. I will
be faithful to you and make you mine, and you will
finally know me as the LORD."   HOSEA 2:16, 19-20

See how very much our Father loves us, for he calls us
his children.   1 JOHN 3:1

Jesus replied, "'You must love the Lord your God
with all your heart, all your soul, and all your mind.'"
                                              MATTHEW 22:37

Drink water from your own well—share your
love only with your wife. . . . May you always be
captivated by her love.   PROVERBS 5:15, 19

$\mathcal{G}$od created you for intimacy; he built into you a long-ing for relationship. The risks of being vulnerable are worth the rewards. When two people have intimacy, they are able to communicate heart to heart, mind to mind, soul to soul. Relational intimacy allows you to openly share all of your burdens, fears, and joys with someone else. Physical intimacy, which is reserved for marriage alone, allows a man and a woman to reach new heights of vulnerability and to communicate at the most profound level. The greatest intimacy of all is intimacy with God, which allows you to understand the very heart of God. As you do, all other intimacy in your relationships takes on new and even greater meaning. God is the source of love, and he created you with the ability to love. Therefore, no one knows more about love than God does. Intimacy with God means experiencing his love to the fullest and returning that love to him. The more you allow God to share with you his intimate love, the more you will share his love with others and enjoy more intimate relationships.

DIVINE PROMISE

THE LORD IS CLOSE TO ALL WHO CALL ON HIM,
YES, TO ALL WHO CALL ON HIM IN TRUTH.
Psalm 145:18

Investing

MY QUESTION *for* GOD

How can I be more motivated to invest in spiritual things?

A MOMENT *with* GOD

Give, and you will receive. Your gift will return to you in full—pressed down, shaken together to make room for more, running over, and poured into your lap. The amount you give will determine the amount you get back.   LUKE 6:38

The LORD gave me what I had.   JOB 1:21

Sell your possessions and give to those in need. This will store up treasure for you in heaven! And the purses of heaven never get old or develop holes. Your treasure will be safe; no thief can steal it and no moth can destroy it.   LUKE 12:33

If you give even a cup of cold water to one of the least of my followers, you will surely be rewarded.

MATTHEW 10:42

At its most basic level, giving is investing your possessions or income in the lives of others. At a deeper level, giving is investing yourself in others. Giving is a remarkable concept. It originates in the heart of a giving God, a God who invests more blessings in his people than we deserve or expect. God invests in you through his gifts of life, love, salvation, and eternity in heaven—all investments he makes in order to have a relationship with you. These gifts are priceless and can be reinvested in the lives of others. In fact, your very character is a reflection of how much you have invested of yourself with God and others. One unique promise of the Bible is that the more you give, the more you receive—not necessarily in material possessions, but in spiritual and eternal rewards. This is a truth that can only be learned by doing. Your monetary investments will become worthless to you when you die—you can't take them with you. But any spiritual investments you make will impact you for eternity.

Divine Promise

THIS WORLD IS FADING AWAY, ALONG WITH EVERYTHING THAT PEOPLE CRAVE. BUT ANYONE WHO DOES WHAT PLEASES GOD WILL LIVE FOREVER.   *1 John 2:17*

Joy

My Questions *for* God

If God promises me joy, does that mean I'll always be happy? What if I don't feel happy?

A Moment *with* God

The apostles left the high council rejoicing that God had counted them worthy to suffer disgrace for the name of Jesus.   Acts 5:41

Since we have been made right in God's sight by faith, we have peace with God because of what Jesus Christ our Lord has done for us. Because of our faith, Christ has brought us into this place of undeserved privilege where we now stand, and we confidently and joyfully look forward to sharing God's glory.   ROMANS 5:1-2

They are being tested by many troubles, and they are very poor. But they are also filled with abundant joy, which has overflowed in rich generosity.

                                        2 CORINTHIANS 8:2

Always be full of joy in the Lord. I say it again— rejoice! . . . I know how to live on almost nothing or with everything.   PHILIPPIANS 4:4, 12

When troubles come your way, consider it an opportunity for great joy.   JAMES 1:2

There is a difference between joy and happiness. Happiness, which is temporary, is a reaction to events in your life. Joy, which is strong and lasting, happens in spite of your circumstances. This kind of joy can only happen by following God and living according to his principles. Happiness that is based on events is not bad; but if it's all you can count on, you will always need to experience happy events to keep you going. Those who know the joy that comes from God don't need events to keep them happy. They develop an inner joy in spite of their circumstances. They know that no matter what happens, God offers hope and promise. Joy is celebrating your walk with God. It is having peace with

God. It is realizing how privileged you are to know
Jesus as your Savior, to have your sins forgiven, to be
friends with God Almighty, and to be certain you will
live forever with him in heaven. It is experiencing the
dramatic change that occurs in your life when you allow the Holy Spirit to control your heart and mind.
God does not promise constant happiness; in fact, the
Bible assures us that we will have problems because we
live in a fallen world. But God does promise lasting joy
to those who follow him. This kind of joy stays with
you despite your problems because you know that God
is with you, that he will help you through them, and
that one day he will take them all away. You can have
this lasting joy even when you don't feel happy.

DIVINE PROMISE

NOW ALL GLORY TO GOD, WHO IS ABLE TO KEEP
YOU FROM FALLING AWAY AND WILL BRING
YOU WITH GREAT JOY INTO HIS GLORIOUS
PRESENCE WITHOUT A SINGLE FAULT. *Jude 1:24*

Kindness

MY QUESTION *for* GOD

I think I'm kind. What does the Bible say kindness looks like?

A MOMENT *with* GOD

There was a believer in Joppa named Tabitha (which in Greek is Dorcas). She was always doing kind things for others and helping the poor.   ACTS 9:36

*K*indness is not just a single act—it's a lifestyle. Begin by showing kindness in the little things you do and say; eventually you will learn to be kind in all situations.

If you see your neighbor's ox or sheep or goat wandering away, don't ignore your responsibility. Take it back to its owner. . . . If you see that your neighbor's donkey or ox has collapsed on the road, do not look the other way. Go and help your neighbor get it back on its feet!   DEUTERONOMY 22:1, 4

*K*indness is not looking the other way or ignoring the needs around you; kindness is attentive to the needs of others and responds sensitively to them.

The people of the island were very kind to us. It was cold and rainy, so they built a fire on the shore to welcome us.   ACTS 28:2

*K*indness is looking for opportunities to help other people.

Make allowance for each other's faults, and forgive anyone who offends you. Remember, the Lord forgave you, so you must forgive others. COLOSSIANS 3:13

Don't repay evil for evil. Don't retaliate with insults when people insult you. Instead, pay them back with a blessing. That is what God has called you to do, and he will bless you for it.   1 PETER 3:9

*K*indness is showing forgiveness and mercy to others, even if they don't deserve it.

John replied, "If you have two shirts, give one to the poor. If you have food, share it with those who are hungry."   LUKE 3:11

Don't forget to show hospitality to strangers, for some who have done this have entertained angels without realizing it!   HEBREWS 13:2

*K*indness is generously sharing what you have with others, even people you don't know.

A servant of the Lord must not quarrel but must be kind to everyone, be able to teach, and be patient with difficult people.   2 TIMOTHY 2:24

*K*indness is teaching others by your example to be peace-loving and patient.

Don't use foul or abusive language. Let everything you say be good and helpful, so that your words will be an encouragement to those who hear them.
                                              EPHESIANS 4:29

*K*indness is using encouraging and helpful words rather than offensive or critical words.

Masters, treat your slaves in the same way. Don't threaten them; remember, you both have the same Master in heaven, and he has no favorites. EPHESIANS 6:9

*K*indness is using your authority appropriately, not abusing it.

If you give even a cup of cold water to one of the least of my followers, you will surely be rewarded.

MATTHEW 10:42

*K*indness is not necessarily a major, award-winning event. God sees and rewards every act of kindness, even small ones.

DIVINE PROMISE

THE LORD IS RIGHTEOUS IN EVERYTHING HE DOES; HE IS FILLED WITH KINDNESS. *Psalm 145:17*

Letting Go

MY QUESTION *for* GOD

I'm having a hard time letting go of certain things. How can I learn to trust God with them?

A MOMENT *with* GOD

Pharaoh gave this order to all his people: "Throw
every newborn Hebrew boy into the Nile River. But
you may let the girls live." About this time, a man
and woman from the tribe of Levi got married. The
woman became pregnant and gave birth to a son. She
saw that he was a special baby and kept him hidden
for three months. But when she could no longer hide
him, she got a basket made of papyrus reeds and
waterproofed it with tar and pitch. She put the baby
in the basket and laid it among the reeds along the
bank of the Nile River. The baby's sister then stood
at a distance, watching to see what would happen to
him. Soon Pharaoh's daughter came down to bathe
in the river, and her attendants walked along the
riverbank. When the princess saw the basket among
the reeds, she sent her maid to get it for her. When
the princess opened it, she saw the baby. The little
boy was crying, and she felt sorry for him. "This must
be one of the Hebrew children," she said. Then the
baby's sister approached the princess. "Should I go
and find one of the Hebrew women to nurse the baby
for you?" she asked. "Yes, do!" the princess replied.
So the girl went and called the baby's mother. "Take
this baby and nurse him for me," the princess told the
baby's mother. "I will pay you for your help." So the
woman took her baby home and nursed him.

EXODUS 1:22–2:9

Pharaoh's threat put all of the Israelites' male children in grave danger. Moses' parents cared for him as long as they could, but then they literally had to let him go. They put him in God's care as they placed him in the basket. They provide us with an example of trusting God in situations that are beyond our control. Do what you know is right for as long as you can; then trust God to take it from there. The more you hold on and try to control every situation, the less you hold on to God. Letting go means that sometimes you serve God by obediently standing aside and watching him work. Moses' mother physically let go of her baby when she placed the basket in the water, but she did not let go of her care and concern for him. Because she trusted in God, he gave her the opportunity to do more for her son than she ever could have hoped for. Letting go does not mean giving up. It means allowing God to make the next move. So if God says stand and watch, then stand by and watch him work! If he says move, then move with him. Either way, it is a divine moment of obedience and service.

DIVINE PROMISE

CALL ON ME WHEN YOU ARE IN TROUBLE,
AND I WILL RESCUE YOU, AND YOU WILL GIVE
ME GLORY. *Psalm 50:15*

Limitations

MY QUESTION *for* GOD

Can God actually use my limitations to accomplish something?

A MOMENT *with* GOD

After sending them home, [Jesus] went up into the hills by himself to pray. Night fell while he was there alone. Meanwhile, the disciples were in trouble far away from land, for a strong wind had risen, and they were fighting heavy waves. About three o'clock in the morning Jesus came toward them, walking on the water. When the disciples saw him walking on the water, they were terrified. In their fear, they cried out, "It's a ghost!" But Jesus spoke to them at once. "Don't be afraid," he said. "Take courage. I am here!" Then Peter called to him, "Lord, if it's really you, tell me to come to you, walking on the water." "Yes, come," Jesus said. So Peter went over the side of the boat and walked on the water toward Jesus. But when he saw the strong wind and the waves, he was terrified and began to sink. "Save me, Lord!" he shouted. Jesus immediately reached out and grabbed him. "You have so little faith," Jesus said. "Why did you doubt me?"   MATTHEW 14:23-31

The portrait of Peter that comes to life in the pages of the New Testament reveals a man of considerable courage and confidence. He was a man's man. At a moment's notice he would pick up a sword or, as in this case, jump into a stormy sea. But in this incident,

Peter came face-to-face with his limitations. Walking on water was one thing Peter could not do on his own. As he felt himself slipping beneath the waves, he cried out, "Save me, Lord!" Immediately he found himself upheld by Jesus' hand. This is a wonderful picture of salvation. Like Peter, you have to face your inability to save yourself. You must pray, "Save me, Lord!" Then you experience a divine moment when Jesus reaches out and pulls you to safety.

DIVINE PROMISE
ALL GLORY TO GOD, WHO IS ABLE, THROUGH HIS MIGHTY POWER AT WORK WITHIN US, TO ACCOMPLISH INFINITELY MORE THAN WE MIGHT ASK OR THINK.   *Ephesians 3:20*

Limitations

MY QUESTION *for* GOD
What does God think when he sees all my faults and limitations?

A MOMENT *with* GOD
The angel of the LORD came and sat beneath the great tree at Ophrah, which belonged to Joash of the clan of Abiezer. Gideon son of Joash was threshing wheat at the bottom of a winepress to hide the grain from the Midianites. The angel of the LORD appeared to him and said, "Mighty hero, the LORD is with you!"

JUDGES 6:11-12

The angel of the Lord greeted Gideon by calling him "mighty hero." Was God talking to the right person? This was Gideon—the guy who was hiding in a winepress from his enemies, the guy who claimed to be the least in his whole family (v. 15). Yet God called him a mighty hero. God's message to Gideon—and to you—is clear: You are more than what you appear to be or what you think you are. God calls out the best in you. He sees more in you than you see in yourself. You may look at your limitations, but God looks at your potential. If you want to increase your opportunities, learn to see life from God's perspective. He doesn't put nearly as many limitations on you as you put on yourself. He sees within you the person he created you to be. How encouraging—the almighty God of the universe sees you for what you can become rather than for what you are! Don't hide because of your limitations; allow God to give you a divine moment by using you in spite of them.

DIVINE PROMISE

EACH TIME [THE LORD] SAID, "MY GRACE IS ALL YOU NEED. MY POWER WORKS BEST IN WEAKNESS." SO NOW I AM GLAD TO BOAST ABOUT MY WEAKNESSES, SO THAT THE POWER OF CHRIST CAN WORK THROUGH ME.

2 Corinthians 12:9

Loneliness

MY QUESTION *for* GOD

I often feel alone when I face difficulties in my life. Where is God during those times?

A MOMENT *with* GOD

When the Ishmaelites, who were Midianite traders, came by, Joseph's brothers pulled him out of the cistern and sold him to them for twenty pieces of silver. . . . The LORD was with Joseph, giving him success in everything he did.   GENESIS 37:28; 39:3

We are hunted down, but never abandoned by God. We get knocked down, but we are not destroyed.

2 CORINTHIANS 4:9

*T*hough you may not feel God's presence or be able to see him working in your life, you can be sure that he is always with you. Many heroes of the Bible felt alone at times, so you should not be surprised when it happens to you. Remember that you often grow the most during times when your faith is challenged. God has a plan to accomplish good out of everything, even your loneliness. If you keep trusting him, you will be assured of his presence and begin to see his plan for you unfold.

DIVINE PROMISE
THE LORD WILL NOT ABANDON HIS PEOPLE.
1 Samuel 12:22

Loss

My Question *for* God

How can I deal with loss in my life?

A Moment *with* God

"Where have you put him?" he asked them. They
told him, "Lord, come and see." Then Jesus wept.
The people who were standing nearby said, "See how
much he loved him!"

John 11:34-36

*D*on't deny your loss. The tears Jesus shed over the
death of Lazarus validate your own tears of grief.

The Egyptians mourned his death for seventy days.

Genesis 50:3

*G*rief over loss is a process that should not be denied
or hurried. The rituals of wakes, visitations, funer-
als, and memorial services all help you move through
the stages of grief. Even if your loss does not involve
death—for example, a friend moved away, a relationship was broken, a good job was lost—you still need
to allow yourself to grieve in order to bring healing to
your soul.

In the spring of the year, when kings normally go out
to war, David sent Joab and the Israelite army to fight
the Ammonites. They destroyed the Ammonite army
and laid siege to the city of Rabbah. However, David

stayed behind in Jerusalem. Late one afternoon,
after his midday rest, David got out of bed and was
walking on the roof of the palace. As he looked out
over the city, he noticed a woman of unusual beauty
taking a bath. He sent someone to find out who
she was.   2 SAMUEL 11:1-3

*F*or reasons unknown, King David gave up the active
leadership of his troops. This loss may have created a
vacuum in his life, which he sought to fill by engag-
ing in an immoral relationship with Bathsheba. As you
grieve over your losses, be careful not to medicate your
pain in ways that only create more pain.

Job stood up and tore his robe in grief. . . . He said, "
. . . The LORD gave me what I had, and the LORD has
taken it away."   JOB 1:20-22

*L*oss always brings pain. Recognizing and expressing
your feelings of pain is not wrong or sinful; rather, it is
honest and appropriate.

The thought of my suffering and homelessness is
bitter beyond words. I will never forget this awful
time, as I grieve over my loss. Yet I still dare to hope
when I remember this: The faithful love of the LORD
never ends! His mercies never cease. Great is his
faithfulness; his mercies begin afresh each morning.

                                 LAMENTATIONS 3:19-23

*T*hose who know God grieve with hope and with the assurance of God's love. Those who don't know God grieve without hope and without help.

You suffered along with those who were thrown into jail, and when all you owned was taken from you, you accepted it with joy. You knew there were better things waiting for you that will last forever.

HEBREWS 10:34

*I*t is important to allow yourself to grieve, but there is a time for grieving to end. You can begin to find healing by serving God and other people with all the energy and enthusiasm you can muster. As a Christian, you have the comfort of knowing that one day you will be with God in heaven, where all grief and loss will be gone forever.

DIVINE PROMISE

THE LORD IS CLOSE TO THE BROKENHEARTED;
HE RESCUES THOSE WHOSE SPIRITS
ARE CRUSHED.   *Psalm 34:18*

Love

MY QUESTION *for* GOD

How do I love God with all my heart, soul, and strength?

A MOMENT *with* GOD

You must love the LORD your God with all your
heart, all your soul, and all your strength.

DEUTERONOMY 6:5

I love the LORD because he hears my voice and my
prayer for mercy.   PSALM 116:1

When you obey my commandments, you remain
in my love. . . . I have told you these things so
that you will be filled with my joy. Yes, your joy
will overflow!   JOHN 15:10-11

Love covers a multitude of sins.   1 PETER 4:8

In modern culture love is often defined in romantic
or sentimental terms. According to the Bible, love is
indeed a feeling, but it is also more than that. It is a
commitment that both protects and produces passionate feelings. Because it is a commitment, love is not
dependent on warm feelings alone but on a consistent
and courageous decision to extend yourself for the
well-being of someone else. Loving feelings can produce commitment, but commitment can also produce
loving feelings. Jesus perfectly demonstrated God's
unconditional love for you when he made the loving
commitment to lay down his life to save you from your
sins. When you love God with all your heart, soul, and
strength, you are making a commitment to develop
a relationship with the Creator of the universe, who
loved you first and daily pursues you with his love.

DIVINE PROMISE

THE LORD SAYS, "I WILL RESCUE THOSE WHO
LOVE ME. I WILL PROTECT THOSE WHO TRUST
IN MY NAME. WHEN THEY CALL ON ME, I WILL
ANSWER; I WILL BE WITH THEM IN TROUBLE.
I WILL RESCUE AND HONOR THEM. I WILL
REWARD THEM WITH A LONG LIFE AND GIVE
THEM MY SALVATION." *Psalm 91:14-16*

Love

MY QUESTION *for* GOD

How do I love my neighbors?

A MOMENT *with* GOD

Always judge people fairly. Do not spread slanderous
gossip among your people. Do not stand idly by when
your neighbor's life is threatened. I am the LORD.

LEVITICUS 19:15-16

Now I am giving you a new commandment: Love
each other. Just as I have loved you, you should love
each other. Your love for one another will prove to
the world that you are my disciples. JOHN 13:34-35

If we love each other, God lives in us, and his love is
brought to full expression in us. 1 JOHN 4:12

Love your neighbor as yourself. MATTHEW 22:39

hy did Jesus say to love your neighbor as yourself? Because God knows that our first instinct is to take care of ourselves. If we can learn to meet the needs of others in the same way we meet our own needs, then we will be fulfilling Jesus' command. Caring for others is what loving our neighbor is all about. Every time you show love to others, you are creating a divine moment in which God is touching two hearts—theirs and yours.

DIVINE PROMISE

IT IS GOOD WHEN YOU OBEY THE ROYAL LAW AS FOUND IN THE SCRIPTURES: "LOVE YOUR NEIGHBOR AS YOURSELF." *James 2:8*

Marriage

MY QUESTION *for* GOD

What are some keys to having a strong, happy marriage?

A MOMENT *with* GOD

Choose today whom you will serve. . . . But as for me and my family, we will serve the LORD.   JOSHUA 24:15

Can two people walk together without agreeing on the direction?   AMOS 3:3

*B*eing united in serving the Lord is one key to a strong marriage. As you walk through life with your wife, you must decide together which direction you want to go—toward the eternal destination of heaven or away from it. This is the key to experiencing daily divine moments together.

Rejoice in the wife of your youth. . . . Let her breasts satisfy you always. May you always be captivated by her love.   PROVERBS 5:18-19

*S*exual faithfulness to your wife is another key to a strong and happy marriage. Without faithfulness, there will be no trust or intimacy.

Since they are no longer two but one, let no one split apart what God has joined together.   MATTHEW 19:6

*C*ommitment to stay together no matter what is essential for a strong and lasting marriage. If you leave open the option for splitting up someday, chances are you will. If you don't allow breaking up to be an option, you will be committed to making your marriage work in all circumstances.

We must not just please ourselves. We should help others do what is right and build them up in the Lord.
                                                ROMANS 15:1-2

Self-sacrifice is essential to a strong marriage. This means thinking of your wife's needs and interests ahead of your own. Who wouldn't want to be in a relationship where someone is always meeting your needs?

May God . . . help you live in complete harmony with each other, as is fitting for followers of Christ Jesus. Then all of you can join together with one voice, giving praise and glory to God.   ROMANS 15:5-7

Understand each other's differences and celebrate them. This fosters respect for each other and turns characteristics that might annoy or distract you into unique strengths that interest and help you.

Submit to one another out of reverence for Christ.

EPHESIANS 5:21

Mutual submission in serving one another is one key to a strong marriage.

Confess your sins to each other and pray for each other.   JAMES 5:16

Praying with each other and for each other helps to strengthen your marriage.

Our letters have been straightforward, and there is nothing written between the lines and nothing you can't understand. I hope someday you will fully understand us, even if you don't understand us now.

2 CORINTHIANS 1:13-14

*C*ommunication is necessary for a strong and happy marriage. Since mind-reading is only possible for God, talk to your wife and keep the lines of communication open, even if the conversation is awkward or difficult. Instead of making each other guess what is on your mind, be honest. This will build trust and openness in your relationship.

Reward her for all she has done. Let her deeds publicly declare her praise. PROVERBS 31:31

*R*egular affirmation will enhance feelings of worth in both you and your wife and will help build a strong marriage. Everyone needs to feel valued. Find ways to affirm your wife each day, and you will increase the strength and joy of your marriage.

The husband should fulfill his wife's sexual needs, and the wife should fulfill her husband's needs.

1 CORINTHIANS 7:3

A healthy sexual relationship is important for a strong and happy marriage because it allows you to express intimacy and vulnerability in a way that is different from any other relationship. Through physical intimacy you can share a special closeness that demonstrates your complete openness to one another. This is what sets marriage apart as a committed relationship like no other.

Love is patient and kind. Love is not jealous or boastful or proud or rude. It does not demand its own way. It is not irritable, and it keeps no record of being wronged.   1 CORINTHIANS 13:4-5

*U*nconditional love is essential for a strong marriage. It means doing the right thing even when your spouse hurts you. Consistently demonstrating unconditional love is perhaps the hardest thing to do in marriage (or any human relationship), but it is the most important key to having a great relationship and winning over the heart of your wife.

DIVINE PROMISE

AS THE SCRIPTURES SAY, "A MAN LEAVES HIS FATHER AND MOTHER AND IS JOINED TO HIS WIFE, AND THE TWO ARE UNITED INTO ONE."
Ephesians 5:31

Meaning

MY QUESTION *for* GOD

How can I find more meaning in my life?

A MOMENT *with* GOD

The LORD says, "I will guide you along the best
pathway for your life. I will advise you and watch
over you." PSALM 32:8

Our present troubles are small and won't last very
long. Yet they produce for us a glory that vastly
outweighs them and will last forever! 2 CORINTHIANS 4:17

As a heaven-bound follower of Jesus, you need to put
heaven and earth in proper perspective. Here on earth,
you will live for a hundred years or less. In heaven, a
hundred *million* years is just the beginning! Yet God has
determined that how you live during your short time
on earth will prepare you for heaven. As you focus on
the unique role God has planned for you in eternity,
you will discover meaning in how you live each day
until then.

DIVINE CHALLENGE

I ONCE THOUGHT THESE THINGS WERE
VALUABLE, BUT NOW I CONSIDER THEM
WORTHLESS BECAUSE OF WHAT CHRIST HAS
DONE. YES, EVERYTHING ELSE IS WORTHLESS
WHEN COMPARED WITH THE INFINITE VALUE
OF KNOWING CHRIST JESUS MY LORD. FOR HIS
SAKE I HAVE DISCARDED EVERYTHING ELSE,
COUNTING IT ALL AS GARBAGE, SO THAT I
COULD GAIN CHRIST. *Philippians 3:7-8*

Mercy

MY QUESTIONS for GOD

Why does God show me mercy? How can I learn to be more merciful to others?

A MOMENT with GOD

The LORD was sorry he had ever made them and put them on the earth. It broke his heart.   GENESIS 6:6

God blessed Noah and his sons and told them, "Be fruitful and multiply. Fill the earth."   GENESIS 9:1

The LORD is compassionate and merciful, slow to get angry and filled with unfailing love. He will not constantly accuse us, nor remain angry forever. He does not punish us for all our sins; he does not deal harshly with us, as we deserve.   PSALM 103:8-10

God looked at all the evil and violence that reigned on earth before the Flood, and it broke his heart. After the Flood, God blessed Noah and told him and his sons to multiply and fill the earth. Why would God want to risk having the same thing happen all over again? Because of his mercy and love. God's mercy gives us a second chance even when we don't deserve it. God's amazing love for us is the reason he is so merciful. God chooses to show mercy to those he loves and who love him. Even though our sin and rebellion against God deserve his punishment; he offers us forgiveness and eternal life instead. When you understand that you don't deserve

God's mercy but he gives it to you anyway, then you will experience a divine moment in which you feel the full impact of God's love for you. Only then will you be able to truly love others and show them mercy, even when they don't deserve it. The mercy you show them will be a reflection of God's unconditional love.

DIVINE PROMISE

WHEN GOD OUR SAVIOR REVEALED HIS KINDNESS AND LOVE, HE SAVED US, NOT BECAUSE OF THE RIGHTEOUS THINGS WE HAD DONE, BUT BECAUSE OF HIS MERCY. HE WASHED AWAY OUR SINS, GIVING US A NEW BIRTH AND NEW LIFE THROUGH THE HOLY SPIRIT. HE GENEROUSLY POURED OUT THE SPIRIT UPON US THROUGH JESUS CHRIST OUR SAVIOR. BECAUSE OF HIS GRACE HE DECLARED US RIGHTEOUS AND GAVE US CONFIDENCE THAT WE WILL INHERIT ETERNAL LIFE. THIS IS A TRUSTWORTHY SAYING. *Titus 3:4-8*

Mistakes

MY QUESTION *for* GOD

With all the mistakes I've made, why doesn't God give up on me?

A MOMENT *with* GOD

Abraham introduced his wife, Sarah, by saying, "She is my sister." So King Abimelech of Gerar sent for Sarah and had her brought to him at his palace.

GENESIS 20:2

Abram believed the LORD, and the LORD counted
him as righteous because of his faith.   GENESIS 15:6

*A*bram made many mistakes. So how could God call
him righteous? Despite his bad choices, Abram believed and trusted in God. It was faith, not perfection,
that made him right in God's eyes. The same principle
is true for you. Rather than looking for goodness, God
is looking for faith and a willingness to follow him.

Finally, Samson shared his secret with her. . . . So the
Philistines captured him and gouged out his eyes. . . .
Then Samson prayed to the LORD, "Sovereign LORD,
remember me again."   JUDGES 16:17, 21, 28

*S*amson's life was filled with foolish mistakes, but he
was still used mightily by God. If God would refuse
to use his people because they make mistakes, no one
would ever accomplish anything for him.

So when the Aramean chariot commanders saw
Jehoshaphat in his royal robes, they went after him.
"There is the king of Israel!" they shouted. But
Jehoshaphat called out, and the LORD saved him. God
helped him by turning the attackers away from him.
As soon as the chariot commanders realized he was
not the king of Israel, they stopped chasing him.

                              2 CHRONICLES 18:31-32

*G*od still helped Jehoshaphat even though he had made the mistake of ignoring the warnings of the prophet Micaiah. If you ask him, God will help you even though you've made mistakes.

Peter swore, "A curse on me if I'm lying—I don't know the man!"   MATTHEW 26:74

*A*fter Peter made the painful, devastating mistake of outrightly denying Jesus, Jesus restored him and used him to build the church. Following Jesus means allowing him to forgive your mistakes and help you work toward a better future.

After looking in all directions to make sure no one was watching, Moses killed the Egyptian and hid the body in the sand.   EXODUS 2:12

It was by faith that Moses left the land of Egypt, not fearing the king's anger. He kept right on going because he kept his eyes on the one who is invisible.

                                                    HEBREWS 11:27

*E*ven Moses' life was marred by a terrible mistake, but the Bible describes his life as one of utmost faith in God.

Jonah got up and went in the opposite direction to get away from the LORD. . . . Now the LORD had arranged for a great fish to swallow Jonah. And Jonah was inside the fish for three days and three nights.

. . . Then the LORD ordered the fish to spit Jonah out
onto the beach. . . . Then the LORD spoke to Jonah
a second time: "Get up and go to the great city of
Nineveh, and deliver the message I have given you."

JONAH 1:3, 17; 2:10; 3:1-2

*O*ne of the worst mistakes you can make is running
away from God. Yet God pursued Jonah and gave him
another chance.

Zechariah said to the angel, "How can I be sure this
will happen? I'm an old man now, and my wife is also
well along in years."   LUKE 1:18

*G*od did not disqualify Zechariah from participating in
his plan just because he had doubts. Instead, he allowed
Zechariah to become the father of John the Baptist.

If we confess our sins to him, he is faithful and
just to forgive us our sins and to cleanse us from
all wickedness.   1 JOHN 1:9

*W*hen your mistakes result in sin, confess your sin to
God. He will forgive you completely.

DIVINE PROMISE

I DON'T MEAN TO SAY THAT I HAVE ALREADY
ACHIEVED THESE THINGS OR THAT I HAVE
ALREADY REACHED PERFECTION. BUT I PRESS
ON TO POSSESS THAT PERFECTION FOR WHICH
CHRIST JESUS FIRST POSSESSED ME. . . . I FOCUS
ON THIS ONE THING: FORGETTING THE PAST
AND LOOKING FORWARD TO WHAT LIES
AHEAD, I PRESS ON TO REACH THE END OF
THE RACE AND RECEIVE THE HEAVENLY PRIZE
FOR WHICH GOD, THROUGH CHRIST JESUS,
IS CALLING US.   *Philippians 3:12-14*

Motivation

MY QUESTION *for* GOD

*How can I be motivated to make the most of the
opportunities that come along?*

A MOMENT *with* GOD

Make the most of every opportunity in these evil days.

EPHESIANS 5:16

A hard worker has plenty of food, but a person who
chases fantasies has no sense.   PROVERBS 12:11

In the meantime, I will be staying here at Ephesus
until the Festival of Pentecost. There is a wide-open
door for a great work here.   1 CORINTHIANS 16:8-9

*W*hen you believe that God is presenting you with an opportunity, respond quickly and work hard to maximize what God has put before you. Be willing to change your plans in order to take advantage of any God-given opportunity. You will be motivated when you think about how God could use you because you've made yourself available for his work. Continue to keep your eyes open for what God will send your way.

DIVINE PROMISE

WE MUST QUICKLY CARRY OUT THE TASKS
ASSIGNED US BY THE ONE WHO SENT US.
THE NIGHT IS COMING, AND THEN NO ONE
CAN WORK.   *John 9:4*

Obedience

MY QUESTION *for* GOD

*Total obedience to God is impossible, so how much must
I obey in order to please him?*

A MOMENT *with* GOD

Obey me, and I will be your God, and you will be my people. Do everything as I say, and all will be well!

JEREMIAH 7:23

Moses said, "This is what the LORD has commanded you to do so that the glory of the LORD may appear to you."

LEVITICUS 9:6

If you look carefully into the perfect law that sets you free, and if you do what it says and don't forget what you heard, then God will bless you for doing it.

JAMES 1:25

God knows you can't obey him completely, so he is more interested in how much you *want* to obey him. To want to obey him more, you must grasp a true understanding of obedience and how it builds or destroys relationships. From the six-year-old who leaves her playmates because her mother has called her in for dinner to the business executive who pays his taxes on time, we all live in a web of relationships that depend upon obedience to authority. Like a loving parent or a responsible government, God sets standards of behavior for your own good and to protect you from evil and harm. Some people defy authority, but obedience actually frees us to enjoy life as God intended because it keeps us from becoming entangled in harmful situations. Even though God's commandments are sometimes difficult to obey or don't always make sense from our human perspective, obedience to him will always bring blessing, joy, and peace. When you look at obedience this way, then you will obey God out of love and gratitude for all he's trying to do for you rather than out of fear of being punished. The more you obey out of love, the more you will want to obey, and the more obedience will become a lifestyle rather than a chore. Since God is the creator of life, he knows how life is supposed to work. Obedience to his ways demonstrates your trust that God's way is best and that it will work for you.

DIVINE PROMISE

OH, THE JOYS OF THOSE WHO DO NOT FOLLOW
THE ADVICE OF THE WICKED, OR STAND
AROUND WITH SINNERS, OR JOIN IN WITH
MOCKERS. BUT THEY DELIGHT IN THE LAW OF
THE LORD, MEDITATING ON IT DAY AND NIGHT.
THEY ARE LIKE TREES PLANTED ALONG THE
RIVERBANK, BEARING FRUIT EACH SEASON.
THEIR LEAVES NEVER WITHER, AND THEY
PROSPER IN ALL THEY DO.   *Psalm 1:1-3*

Opportunities

MY QUESTION *for* GOD

How can I prepare for opportunities before they come?

A MOMENT *with* GOD

Philip ran over and heard the man reading from the
prophet Isaiah. Philip asked, "Do you understand
what you are reading?"   ACTS 8:30

Make the most of every opportunity in these evil days.
                                              EPHESIANS 5:16

God regularly places divine moments right in front of
you—opportunities to do good, to help someone in
need, or to tell someone about God. Always be on the
lookout for these opportunities to share your faith in
word or deed. God will put them in front of you; you
simply need to act on them.

Because of my imprisonment, most of the believers
here have gained confidence and boldly speak God's
message without fear.   PHILIPPIANS 1:14

*W*hen you see an opportunity to do good, jump at it.
The more you sit back and think about it, the less likely
you are to act. Even if you are experiencing personal
hardship, helping others can be therapeutic.

Potiphar . . . made Joseph his personal attendant.
He put him in charge of his entire household and
everything he owned. . . . With Joseph there, he
didn't worry about a thing.   GENESIS 39:4, 6

They replied, "We both had dreams last night, but
no one can tell us what they mean." "Interpreting
dreams is God's business," Joseph replied. "Go ahead
and tell me your dreams."   GENESIS 40:8

*A*cting responsibly will open doors of opportunity.
How you handle the responsibilities you've been given
determines whether or not you will be trusted with
more. Joseph was sold into slavery by his own brothers.
He could have whined and complained, become bitter
and given up. Instead, he seized every opportunity to
do good and be helpful. As a result, he quickly became
trusted for his integrity and eventually rose to great
prominence in Egypt.

Meanwhile, the believers who had been scattered
during the persecution after Stephen's death traveled

as far as Phoenicia, Cyprus, and Antioch of Syria.
They preached the word of God.   ACTS 11:19

*S*ee unexpected changes or difficulties as opportunities to serve God.

Where can we go? Our brothers have demoralized us
with their report.   DEUTERONOMY 1:28

*D*on't let fear or doubt cause you to miss opportunities that are from God. God often sends opportunities
that require faith and courage so that you will learn to
trust him.

DIVINE PROMISE

TO THOSE WHO USE WELL WHAT THEY ARE
GIVEN, EVEN MORE WILL BE GIVEN, AND THEY
WILL HAVE AN ABUNDANCE. BUT FROM THOSE
WHO DO NOTHING, EVEN WHAT LITTLE THEY
HAVE WILL BE TAKEN AWAY. *Matthew 25:29*

Opposition

MY QUESTION *for* GOD

*Why do I encounter so much opposition when I am just
trying to do what God wants?*

A MOMENT *with* GOD

The local residents tried to discourage and frighten the people of Judah to keep them from their work. They bribed agents to work against them and to frustrate their plans. This went on during the entire reign of King Cyrus of Persia and lasted until King Darius of Persia took the throne.   EZRA 4:4-5

If you are being faithful to God, you can expect persistent opposition from those who don't want to see God's work succeed. In Ezra's account of the Israelites' rebuilding of the Temple, those who opposed God, God's people, and God's work persisted in trying to stop them for almost two decades! God's adversaries don't quit after one or two attempts to defeat you. This is true of both human opposition and spiritual opposition. Satan is the enemy of your soul. You must therefore strengthen yourself for a lifelong campaign against the forces of darkness. Dashed expectations of easy success will breed frustration and despair. But the expectation of extended conflict will lead to careful preparation and patient determination. Never forget that no matter how long the battle, victory belongs to the Lord! When you face opposition, rejoice that you are living so effectively for God that his enemies are taking notice. Then look at each battle as an opportunity to experience a divine moment of victory.

DIVINE PROMISE

GOD BLESSES THOSE WHO ARE PERSECUTED
FOR DOING RIGHT, FOR THE KINGDOM OF
HEAVEN IS THEIRS. GOD BLESSES YOU WHEN
PEOPLE MOCK YOU AND PERSECUTE YOU AND
LIE ABOUT YOU AND SAY ALL SORTS OF EVIL
THINGS AGAINST YOU BECAUSE YOU ARE MY
FOLLOWERS. BE HAPPY ABOUT IT! BE VERY
GLAD! FOR A GREAT REWARD AWAITS YOU
IN HEAVEN.   *Matthew 5:10-12*

Pain

MY QUESTION *for* GOD

How can I handle painful situations in my life?

A MOMENT *with* GOD

We believers also groan, even though we have the
Holy Spirit within us as a foretaste of future glory,
for we long for our bodies to be released from sin and
suffering. We, too, wait with eager hope for the day
when God will give us our full rights as his adopted
children, including the new bodies he has promised
us. We were given this hope when we were saved. (If
we already have something, we don't need to hope for
it. But if we look forward to something we don't yet
have, we must wait patiently and confidently.)

ROMANS 8:23-25

God himself will be with them. He will wipe every tear from their eyes, and there will be no more death or sorrow or crying or pain. All these things are gone forever.   REVELATION 21:3-4

$\mathscr{T}$rusting God does not produce a storybook life in which every problem is quickly resolved. Sometimes people get sick and don't get better; relationships break down and can't be restored; jobs are lost and not regained. You can rejoice, however, that you are assured of a happy ending. When Jesus returns, discomfort, disappointment, disease, pain, and death will disappear, and you will live with joy in God's presence forever. Because this happy ending is utterly certain, you can endure the unanswered questions and unending crises of this life. Sometimes it's hard to see God in the pain of the present. When you go through times like that, look forward to God's promise of an eternally pain-free future. It will give you a powerful dose of hope to help you through the present.

DIVINE PROMISE

YOU HAVE TURNED MY MOURNING INTO JOYFUL DANCING. YOU HAVE TAKEN AWAY MY CLOTHES OF MOURNING AND CLOTHED ME WITH JOY, THAT I MIGHT SING PRAISES TO YOU AND NOT BE SILENT. *Psalm 30:11-12*

Passion

MY QUESTION *for* GOD

I used to be on fire for God. Why can't I seem to keep that passion?

A MOMENT *with* GOD

King Solomon loved many foreign women. . . . The LORD had clearly instructed the people of Israel, "You must not marry them, because they will turn your hearts to their gods." Yet Solomon insisted on loving them anyway. . . . And in fact, they did turn his heart away from the LORD.   1 KINGS 11:1-3

When sin gets a foothold in your life, it always leads you away from God. It squelches your passion and produces an apathetic attitude toward God. Satan will use all his power to keep you from getting excited about following God.

The woman was convinced. She saw that the tree was beautiful and its fruit looked delicious, and she wanted the wisdom it would give her. So she took some of the fruit and ate it. Then she gave some to her husband, who was with her, and he ate it, too.

GENESIS 3:6

Temptation takes your focus off God and makes something else seem more exciting. Perhaps you do not make a conscious decision to move away from God, but something else suddenly gets your attention. If what you become excited about is not what God wants you to do, your passion for God will quickly die.

They went to the olive grove called Gethsemane, and Jesus said, "Sit here while I go and pray." . . . He went on a little farther and fell to the ground. He prayed. . . . Then he returned and found the disciples asleep. He said to Peter, "Simon, are you asleep? Couldn't you watch with me even one hour? Keep watch and pray, so that you will not give in to temptation. For the spirit is willing, but the body is weak."

MARK 14:32, 35-38

*S*ometimes you're just too tired or unaware to see the significance of what is going on around you. You must be passionate about looking for God in every circumstance.

You must continue to believe this truth and stand firmly in it. Don't drift away from the assurance you received when you heard the Good News. The Good News has been preached all over the world, and I, Paul, have been appointed as God's servant to proclaim it.   COLOSSIANS 1:23

We must listen very carefully to the truth we have heard, or we may drift away from it.   HEBREWS 2:1

I have this complaint against you. You don't love me or each other as you did at first!   REVELATION 2:4

$\mathcal{L}$ike all relationships, your relationship with God takes effort and energy. God is always fully committed to you. For your relationship with God to be exciting, you must be fully committed to him. Be diligent in your efforts to get to know him better. Here are three strategies for doing that: Consistently study God's Word, cultivate a thankful heart, and engage in acts of service to others. This will help fight off feelings of apathy toward God and renew your passion for the purpose he has for your life. You will again be excited about the blessings he has given you and has promised you in the future.

DIVINE PROMISE

I WILL GIVE THEM SINGLENESS OF HEART AND PUT A NEW SPIRIT WITHIN THEM. I WILL TAKE AWAY THEIR STONY, STUBBORN HEART AND GIVE THEM A TENDER, RESPONSIVE HEART.
Ezekiel 11:19

$\mathcal{P}$ast

MY QUESTION *for* GOD

I can't seem to shake some things from my past. Can God help me overcome them?

A MOMENT *with* GOD

When I refused to confess my sin, my body wasted away, and I groaned all day long. Day and night your

hand of discipline was heavy on me. My strength
evaporated like water in the summer heat. Finally,
I confessed all my sins to you and stopped trying to
hide my guilt. I said to myself, "I will confess my
rebellion to the LORD." And you forgave me! All my
guilt is gone.   PSALM 32:3-5

I will delight in your decrees and not forget your
word. . . . I will never forget your commandments,
for by them you give me life.   PSALM 119:16, 93

Though your sins are like scarlet, I will make them
as white as snow. Though they are red like crimson,
I will make them as white as wool.   ISAIAH 1:18

The past is like a photo album containing snapshots
of every moment of your life. These snapshots show
not just your happy moments and celebrations, but also
your failures, tragedies, and acts of deepest shame.
Most of us would like to lock away some parts of our
past or tear out the snapshots that expose the moments
we'd like to forget. The apostle Paul, one of the greatest men in the New Testament, had a past he wished he
could forget. His album was full of snapshots record-
ing his days of persecuting and killing Christians. Paul
could have been burdened with immense regret, but he
understood that his past had been redeemed through
God's healing and forgiveness. How you view your past
affects how you live in the present and in the future.
Some of us have a past containing a strong spiritual
heritage from loving parents and mentors. Don't take
that for granted; use it to help and minister to others.

Some of us have a past filled with regret over actions that were wrong or hurtful. Some of us have a tragic past marred by abuse, neglect, violence, or the shameful acts of other people. No matter what you've done or what's been done to you, God is ready to forgive you, heal you, cleanse you of sin and guilt, and give you a new start—fully forgiven. God wants to throw away all the bad snapshots and give you a new present and future—and he can if you'll let him. God can remove your regret, guilt, and shame, and you can be free to live in peace with purpose and joy.

DIVINE PROMISE

I WILL FORGIVE THEIR WICKEDNESS, AND I WILL NEVER AGAIN REMEMBER THEIR SINS.
Hebrews 8:12

Patience

MY QUESTION *for* GOD

Why do I have to wait patiently for God to act in my life?

A MOMENT *with* GOD

Then [the angel] said, "Don't be afraid, Daniel. Since the first day you began to pray for understanding and to humble yourself before your God, your request has been heard in heaven. I have come in answer to your prayer. But for twenty-one days the spirit prince of the kingdom of Persia blocked my way." DANIEL 10:12-13

*D*aniel prayed expectantly, but he had to wait for an answer because there was spiritual interference. You may not understand why God's response to your prayers seem delayed, but you can be sure that the Lord will answer. Remember that God hears your every prayer.

We can rejoice, too, when we run into problems and trials, for we know that they help us develop endurance. And endurance develops strength of character, and character strengthens our confident hope of salvation. And this hope will not lead to disappointment. For we know how dearly God loves us, because he has given us the Holy Spirit to fill our hearts with his love.   ROMANS 5:3-5

*T*his world is God's waiting room. While you wait, you learn to trust him. You gain endurance, strength, humility, and a deeper appreciation for God's care.

Supplement your faith with a generous provision of moral excellence, and moral excellence with knowledge, and knowledge with self-control, and self-control with patient endurance, and patient endurance with godliness, and godliness with brotherly affection, and brotherly affection with love for everyone. The more you grow like this, the more productive and useful you will be in your knowledge of our Lord Jesus Christ.   2 PETER 1:6-8

*P*atience is one of the tools God uses to mold you into a vessel fit for his purposes. Your patience grows

into endurance and strength of character. It leads you
to godliness and godly service.

DIVINE PROMISE

THE LORD MUST WAIT FOR YOU TO COME TO
HIM SO HE CAN SHOW YOU HIS LOVE AND
COMPASSION. FOR THE LORD IS A FAITHFUL
GOD. BLESSED ARE THOSE WHO WAIT FOR
HIS HELP.   *Isaiah 30:18*

Peace

MY QUESTION *for* GOD

*With all the upheaval in my life, how can I maintain a sense
of peace?*

A MOMENT *with* GOD

This change of plans greatly upset Jonah, and he
became very angry.   JONAH 4:1

[Lord,] you are always the same.   HEBREWS 1:12

Heaven and earth will disappear, but my words will
never disappear.   MARK 13:31

I am leaving you with a gift—peace of mind and
heart. And the peace I give is a gift the world cannot
give. So don't be troubled or afraid.   JOHN 14:27

$\mathscr{C}$hange is one thing that never changes. You can be sure that you will always face new challenges. Don't be upset, like Jonah, when your plans are thwarted. Instead, build your life on the changeless principles and promises that God gives you in his Word. When you experience upheaval, turn to God's Word to maintain your perspective and stay grounded. Remember the inheritance that awaits you in heaven, beyond change and decay, and you will have peace. It is essential that you approach life with this eternal perspective. It gives you the security of knowing that your future is in God's hands. As an added bonus, you are assured that God's power, comfort, and peace are available to you now.

DIVINE PROMISE

YOU WILL KEEP IN PERFECT PEACE ALL WHO TRUST IN YOU, ALL WHOSE THOUGHTS ARE FIXED ON YOU! *Isaiah 26:3*

Perseverance

MY QUESTION *for* GOD

How do I develop the perseverance to get through tough times?

A MOMENT *with* GOD

We think you ought to know, dear brothers and sisters, about the trouble we went through in the province of Asia. We were crushed and overwhelmed beyond our ability to endure, and we thought we

would never live through it. In fact, we expected to
die. But as a result, we stopped relying on ourselves
and learned to rely only on God, who raises the dead.

2 CORINTHIANS 1:8-9

We also pray that you will be strengthened with all
his glorious power so you will have all the endurance
and patience you need. May you be filled with joy.

COLOSSIANS 1:11

I am certain that God, who began the good work
within you, will continue his work until it is finally
finished on the day when Christ Jesus returns.

PHILIPPIANS 1:6

Dear brothers and sisters, when troubles come your
way, consider it an opportunity for great joy. For you
know that when your faith is tested, your endurance
has a chance to grow.   JAMES 1:2-3

*P*erseverance can be defined as "courage stretched
out." Although God sometimes delivers his people
from difficult or painful circumstances, he often calls
us to courageous and enduring faithfulness in the midst
of trials. According to the Bible, perseverance is not
just enduring difficult situations; it is overcoming them
with obedience, hope, and joy. If you don't learn to
persevere through your struggles, you will fall into the
habit of giving up. But when you persevere until you
come out on the other side, you grow stronger in your
faith. You see the benefits of obeying God, and you de-

velop the confidence that when problems come again, you will get through them with God's help.

DIVINE PROMISE

THE SOVEREIGN LORD IS MY STRENGTH! HE MAKES ME AS SUREFOOTED AS A DEER, ABLE TO TREAD UPON THE HEIGHTS.   *Habakkuk 3:19*

Perspective

MY QUESTION *for* GOD

How do I keep the proper perspective on life?

A MOMENT *with* GOD

The people of Israel said to Moses, "Look, we are doomed! We are dead! We are ruined! Everyone who even comes close to the Tabernacle of the LORD dies. Are we all doomed to die?"   NUMBERS 17:12-13

Martha was distracted by the big dinner she was preparing. She came to Jesus and said, "Lord, doesn't it seem unfair to you that my sister just sits here while I do all the work? Tell her to come and help me." But the Lord said to her, "My dear Martha, you are worried and upset over all these details!"   LUKE 10:40-41

The perspective of the Israelites was completely opposite of reality. Instead of seeing the Tabernacle as a place to worship God, they saw it as a place of fear and judgment. What happened? Their perspective of God himself was wrong because their actions had changed from obedience to disobedience. Thus they set themselves up for the natural and painful consequences of sin. Obeying God helps you keep a proper perspective on life. It keeps you focused on what is really important, it leads you in doing God's will, and it gives you an eternal orientation that impacts the way you live today. When you obey God, you realize that everything you really need is what God already supplies you with in great abundance. When you drift away from consistently obeying God, you lose your perspective. Your actions become selfish, and your thoughts slide toward cynicism and dissatisfaction. If you make God your first priority, he will give you perspective on your activities as well as a desire to obey him. Then you will begin to see the rewards of obedience. Ask God, and he will give you the proper perspective on life.

DIVINE PROMISE

IF YOU TRY TO HANG ON TO YOUR LIFE, YOU WILL LOSE IT. BUT IF YOU GIVE UP YOUR LIFE FOR MY SAKE, YOU WILL SAVE IT. *Matthew 16:25*

Planning

MY QUESTION *for* GOD

If God has a plan, should I do any planning?

A MOMENT *with* GOD

God is telling Pharaoh in advance what he is about to do. . . . Joseph's suggestions were well received by Pharaoh and his officials. So Pharaoh asked his officials, "Can we find anyone else like this man so obviously filled with the spirit of God?"

GENESIS 41:25, 37-38

What you ought to say is, "If the Lord wants us to, we will live and do this or that."   JAMES 4:15

We know that God causes everything to work together for the good of those who love God and are called according to his purpose for them.   ROMANS 8:28

Joseph's willingness to use his God-given gifts to help the Egyptians plan for seven years of famine allowed God's plan to be carried out. It's fine to ask God to bless your plans, but you should also be willing to use your gifts and abilities to help carry out God's plans. What a divine moment it is when God uses you to implement his plan! How do you know what work God wants you to be a part of? The first step is to have an open mind and an obedient heart, like Joseph did. The path of obedience will always take you in the right direction. As you follow God, plan to become a part of his plan.

DIVINE PROMISE

TRUST IN THE LORD WITH ALL YOUR
HEART; DO NOT DEPEND ON YOUR OWN
UNDERSTANDING. SEEK HIS WILL IN ALL YOU
DO, AND HE WILL SHOW YOU WHICH PATH
TO TAKE.   *Proverbs 3:5-6*

Potential

MY QUESTION *for* GOD

How does God help me reach my full potential?

A MOMENT *with* GOD

Gideon . . . was threshing wheat at the bottom of a
winepress to hide the grain from the Midianites. The
angel of the LORD appeared to him and said, "Mighty
hero, the LORD is with you! . . . Go with the strength
you have, and rescue Israel from the Midianites. I
am sending you!" "But LORD," Gideon replied, "how
can I rescue Israel? My clan is the weakest in the
whole tribe of Manasseh, and I am the least in my
entire family!"   JUDGES 6:11-12, 14-15

*T*he angel of the Lord greeted Gideon by calling him
"mighty hero." Was God talking to the right person?
Gideon was hiding from his enemies, and he saw himself as the least in his family. But when God looked at
Gideon, he saw the man who would rescue Israel. In
the same way, God brings out the best in you, and he

sees more in you than you see in yourself. You look at your limitations, but God looks at your potential. He doesn't put nearly as many limitations on you as you put on yourself. God sees in you what he created you to be. You began developing your spiritual potential when you repented of your sin. When you gave God control of your life, the Holy Spirit came to live in your heart. The Spirit helps you reach the spiritual potential for which God created you—to reflect his holiness and to use your gifts to help others.

DIVINE PROMISE
I CAN DO EVERYTHING THROUGH CHRIST,
WHO GIVES ME STRENGTH.   *Philippians 4:13*

Power

MY QUESTION *for* GOD

Can power be dangerous?

A MOMENT *with* GOD

Let's build a great city for ourselves with a tower that reaches into the sky. This will make us famous.

GENESIS 11:4

O Egypt, to which of the trees of Eden will you compare your strength and glory? You, too, will be brought down to the depths with all these other nations. You will lie there among the outcasts who have died by the sword. This will be the fate of

Pharaoh and all his hordes. I, the Sovereign LORD,
have spoken!   EZEKIEL 31:18

*P*ower is intoxicating—with it comes recognition,
control, and often wealth. These feed pride, and pride
leads you away from God and into sin. This is why power
so often corrupts. If you are in a position of power or
authority, two things will help you use it wisely: accountability and service. When you have to explain your
motives to others, you will be more careful about what
you do and say. When you determine to serve others
with your power rather than be served, you will gain
great support and loyalty from those in your care.

DIVINE PROMISE

IT IS NOT THAT WE THINK WE ARE QUALIFIED
TO DO ANYTHING ON OUR OWN. OUR
QUALIFICATION COMES FROM GOD.

2 Corinthians 3:5

Power of God

MY QUESTION *for* GOD

How can I experience God's power working through me?

A MOMENT *with* GOD

I also pray that you will understand the incredible
greatness of God's power for us who believe him.

This is the same mighty power that raised Christ
from the dead and seated him in the place of honor
at God's right hand in the heavenly realms.

EPHESIANS 1:19-20

I work and struggle so hard, depending on Christ's
mighty power that works within me.   COLOSSIANS 1:29

It is not that we think we are qualified to do anything
on our own. Our qualification comes from God.

2 CORINTHIANS 3:5

You must call a meeting of the church. I will be
present with you in spirit, and so will the power of
our Lord Jesus.   1 CORINTHIANS 5:4

I pray that from his glorious, unlimited resources
he will empower you with inner strength through
his Spirit.   EPHESIANS 3:16-17

We now have this light shining in our hearts, but we
ourselves are like fragile clay jars containing this great
treasure. This makes it clear that our great power is
from God, not from ourselves.   2 CORINTHIANS 4:7

Imagine experiencing the earth's strongest earth-
quake, tallest tsunami, wildest volcano, and most devastating hurricane—all at the same time. This cannot
even begin to compare to God's power! He is the creator of all these phenomena, and what is created is never
more powerful than the creator. This same God has the
power to calm the storms in your heart, to dry up a
flood of fear, to quench the lust for sin, and to control

the whirlwind of your life. You must put more trust in God's power than your own. Thankfully, God's power does not depend on human strength. In fact, your resources can get in the way if you rely on them instead of on the Lord. God's power flows through you, especially your weaknesses, like an electric current flows through a wire. The wire is simply a conductor; it has no power in itself. But without the wire, the current doesn't go anywhere. God is looking for people who are willing to be wired for his service. If you are willing, the same power God used to create the world and defeat Satan will be available to you.

DIVINE PROMISE

ALL GLORY TO GOD, WHO IS ABLE, THROUGH HIS MIGHTY POWER AT WORK WITHIN US, TO ACCOMPLISH INFINITELY MORE THAN WE MIGHT ASK OR THINK.   *Ephesians 3:20*

Prayer

MY QUESTION *for* GOD

Does God always answer prayer?

A MOMENT *with* GOD

I love the LORD because he hears my voice and my prayer for mercy.
                                                        PSALM 116:1

Three different times I begged the Lord to take it away. Each time he said, "My grace is all you need. My power works best in weakness." 2 CORINTHIANS 12:8-9

If you remain in me and my words remain in you, you may ask for anything you want, and it will be granted! JOHN 15:7

God listens carefully to every prayer and answers each one. His answer may be yes, no, or wait, just as loving parents might give each of these three responses to the requests of their child. Answering yes to every request would spoil you and endanger your well-being. Answering no to every request would be vindictive, stingy, and hard on your spirit. Answering wait to every request would frustrate you. God always answers your prayers according to what he knows is best for you. Knowing that God always listens and answers should inspire you to pray continually, even if his answer is not always the one you wanted. When you don't get the answer you want, don't interpret it to mean that God hasn't heard you; rather, look for how it might be pointing you in a different direction. You will grow in spiritual maturity as you seek to understand why God's answers to your prayers are in your best interest.

DIVINE PROMISE

THE EYES OF THE LORD WATCH OVER THOSE WHO DO RIGHT, AND HIS EARS ARE OPEN TO THEIR PRAYERS. *1 Peter 3:12*

Prayer

MY QUESTION *for* GOD

What kind of attitude does God want when I communicate with him?

A MOMENT *with* GOD

O my people, trust in him at all times. Pour out your heart to him, for God is our refuge.   PSALM 62:8

Devote yourselves to prayer with an alert mind and a thankful heart.   COLOSSIANS 4:2

Never stop praying.   1 THESSALONIANS 5:17

[Jesus prayed,] "Father, if you are willing, please take this cup of suffering away from me. Yet I want your will to be done, not mine."   LUKE 22:42

[The angel] said, "Don't be afraid, Daniel. Since the first day you began to pray for understanding and to humble yourself before your God, your request has been heard in heaven. I have come in answer to your prayer."   DANIEL 10:12

The Bible teaches that God honors and acknowledges the prayers of the humble. Humility comes when you recognize that you need God. Before you ask with boldness, fall to your knees in humility. When you humbly come to God, it shows that you recognize his sovereignty. Then your prayers will be better aligned with his plans for you. Following God's will for your

life will lead you toward what is good and right and
away from sin and harm.

DIVINE PROMISE

**HUMBLE YOURSELVES UNDER THE MIGHTY
POWER OF GOD, AND AT THE RIGHT TIME HE
WILL LIFT YOU UP IN HONOR.** *1 Peter 5:6*

Preparation

My Question *for* God

How can I prepare for the challenges of life?

A Moment *with* God

Pharaoh sent for Joseph at once, and he was quickly
brought from the prison. After he shaved and changed
his clothes, he went in and stood before Pharaoh. . . .
Joseph's suggestions were well received by Pharaoh
and his officials. So Pharaoh asked his officials, "Can
we find anyone else like this man so obviously filled
with the spirit of God?"   GENESIS 41:14, 37-38

How can you make wise decisions at a moment's
notice? The key is to be prepared by developing wisdom over time. You can't anticipate everything that
might happen in any given day, but when you are prepared spiritually—when you have developed godly
wisdom—you will know the right thing to do so God

can use you to accomplish good. You will be ready to act swiftly and decisively because you have a wellspring of wisdom to draw upon.

If you keep yourself pure, you will be a special utensil for honorable use. Your life will be clean, and you will be ready for the Master to use you for every good work.   2 TIMOTHY 2:21

*P*urity—keeping your heart as clean as possible from the stain of sin—prepares you to be filled with God's wisdom and guidance so you can serve him and be involved in the work he is doing around you.

Guard your heart above all else, for it determines the course of your life.   PROVERBS 4:23

*T*he best time to prepare for temptation is before you meet it face-to-face. Train yourself in quiet times so you will have the spiritual wisdom, strength, and commitment to honor God in the face of intense desires and temptation.

Be strong in the Lord and in his mighty power. Put on all of God's armor so that you will be able to stand firm against all strategies of the devil.   EPHESIANS 6:10-11

*P*repare for spiritual warfare by putting on the defensive armor that God has given you—truth, righteousness, knowledge of the Bible, faith, assurance of salvation, and prayer.

Anyone who eats this bread or drinks this cup of the Lord unworthily is guilty of sinning against the body and blood of the Lord. That is why you should examine yourself before eating the bread and drinking the cup.   1 CORINTHIANS 11:27-28

*P*repare for worship by getting your heart right with God.

Instead, you must worship Christ as Lord of your life. And if someone asks about your Christian hope, always be ready to explain it.   1 PETER 3:15

*A*lways be prepared to explain what you believe about Jesus and why your faith is important to you. With a little preparation, your witness will have a bigger impact.

Don't worry in advance about how to answer the charges against you, for I will give you the right words and such wisdom that none of your opponents will be able to reply or refute you!   LUKE 21:14-15

*P*repare to defend your faith. When attacks come, the Holy Spirit will help you speak with authority and courage. If the Holy Spirit were speaking to you today, would you be able to hear him? Do you know his voice?

Take time each day to stay in touch with the Spirit so you will hear him when he speaks to you.

DIVINE PROMISE

THERE IS MORE THAN ENOUGH ROOM IN
MY FATHER'S HOME. IF THIS WERE NOT
SO, WOULD I HAVE TOLD YOU THAT I AM
GOING TO PREPARE A PLACE FOR YOU? WHEN
EVERYTHING IS READY, I WILL COME AND GET
YOU, SO THAT YOU WILL ALWAYS BE WITH ME
WHERE I AM.   *John 14:2-3*

Presence of God

MY QUESTION *for* GOD

How can I experience God's presence more often in my life?

A MOMENT *with* GOD

The LORD is close to all who call on him, yes, to all who call on him in truth.   PSALM 145:18

The Lord invites you to call on him without hesitation. If you are sincere in wanting to know him—rather than just looking for a good-luck charm or magic genie—God promises to reveal himself to you.

If my people who are called by my name will humble themselves and pray and seek my face and turn from their wicked ways, I will hear from heaven and will forgive their sins.   2 CHRONICLES 7:14

Come close to God, and God will come close to you. Wash your hands, you sinners; purify your hearts, for your loyalty is divided between God and the world.

JAMES 4:8

Sin drives a wedge between you and God. You can experience God's presence again when you turn from your sinful habits and attitudes, confess them to God, and ask him to forgive you and make you clean.

Because of Christ and our faith in him, we can now come boldly and confidently into God's presence.

EPHESIANS 3:12

When Jesus sacrificed his own life for you, dying on the cross to pay the price for your sin, he made it possible for you to come into the presence of God.

When you pray, I will listen. If you look for me wholeheartedly, you will find me. JEREMIAH 29:12-13

Seeking and finding God requires earnest, purposeful prayer.

Keep on asking, and you will receive what you ask for. MATTHEW 7:7

God invites you to approach him often and persistently.

DIVINE PROMISE

I KNOW THE LORD IS ALWAYS WITH ME. I WILL
NOT BE SHAKEN, FOR HE IS RIGHT BESIDE
ME. . . . YOU WILL SHOW ME THE WAY OF LIFE,
GRANTING ME THE JOY OF YOUR PRESENCE
AND THE PLEASURES OF LIVING WITH YOU
FOREVER.   *Psalm 16:8, 11*

Pressure

MY QUESTION *for* GOD

Is pressure ever a good thing?

A MOMENT *with* GOD

I tell you this, you must give an account on judgment
day for every idle word you speak.   MATTHEW 12:36

We are pressed on every side by troubles, but we are
not crushed. We are perplexed, but not driven to
despair. We are hunted down, but never abandoned
by God. We get knocked down, but we are not
destroyed. Through suffering, our bodies continue to
share in the death of Jesus so that the life of Jesus may
also be seen in our bodies.   2 CORINTHIANS 4:8-10

The pressures in your life can be positive or negative. We generally think of peer pressure as a negative
influence, such as when you are swayed by friends or
coworkers to join them in behavior that is contrary to
God's standards for living. But pressure can be posi-

tive, too. For example, the pressure of accountability can be a powerful force for positive change. If a father tells his teenage son to clean up his room or face being grounded from the car for a week, the son will likely be very motivated to accomplish that particular task! Jesus reminds us that we are all accountable for our words and actions. The day is coming when God will judge everything and everyone, and we will receive the good or bad consequences that our actions deserve. This knowledge leads us to renew our commitment to holy living and to seek the forgiveness that only Jesus can offer.

DIVINE PROMISE

OH, THE JOYS OF THOSE WHO DO NOT FOLLOW THE ADVICE OF THE WICKED, OR STAND AROUND WITH SINNERS, OR JOIN IN WITH MOCKERS   *Psalm 1:1*

Pretending

MY QUESTION *for* GOD

How can I make my faith more real, especially among those who don't believe as I do?

A MOMENT *with* GOD

If you see your neighbor's ox or sheep or goat wandering away, don't ignore your responsibility. Take it back to its owner. . . . Do the same if you find

your neighbor's donkey, clothing, or anything else
your neighbor loses.   DEUTERONOMY 22:1, 3

Be careful to live properly among your unbelieving
neighbors. Then even if they accuse you of doing
wrong, they will see your honorable behavior,
and they will give honor to God when he judges
the world.   1 PETER 2:12

Live wisely among those who are not believers,
and make the most of every opportunity. Let your
conversation be gracious and attractive so that you
will have the right response for everyone.

                                        COLOSSIANS 4:5-6

Don't just pretend to love others. Really love them.
Hate what is wrong. Hold tightly to what is good.

                                            ROMANS 12:9

In our world we seem to find it increasingly easy
to say, "I don't want to get involved." When we see
someone in need or notice something we could do to
help others, we may be tempted to turn a blind eye and
pretend we don't notice. We may hope someone else
will do something about it. God reminds us that pretending to care about the needy, or pretending not to
notice when someone needs help, or pretending there's
nothing you can do, are all forms of hypocrisy. Genu-
ine faith is compassionate and active, ready and willing
to go the extra mile to help those in need.

Divine Promise

DEAR CHILDREN, LET'S NOT MERELY SAY THAT
WE LOVE EACH OTHER; LET US SHOW THE
TRUTH BY OUR ACTIONS. OUR ACTIONS WILL
SHOW THAT WE BELONG TO THE TRUTH, SO
WE WILL BE CONFIDENT WHEN WE STAND
BEFORE GOD.   *1 John 3:18-19*

Pride

My Question *for* God

How can I tell if I am struggling with pride?

A Moment *with* God

Pharaoh summoned Moses and Aaron and begged,
"Plead with the LORD to take the frogs away from
me and my people. I will let your people go, so they
can offer sacrifices to the LORD." . . . So Moses
and Aaron left Pharaoh's palace, and Moses cried
out to the LORD about the frogs he had inflicted on
Pharaoh. And the LORD did just what Moses had
predicted. The frogs in the houses, the courtyards,
and the fields all died. The Egyptians piled them into
great heaps, and a terrible stench filled the land. But
when Pharaoh saw that relief had come, he became
stubborn. He refused to listen to Moses and Aaron,
just as the LORD had predicted.   EXODUS 8:8, 12-15

With each plague that God sent upon Egypt, Pharaoh weakened—but only temporarily. Over time Pharaoh tried to negotiate a number of compromises to let Israel go—but without actually setting them free. He tried to maintain control because he refused to acknowledge the sovereign authority of Israel's God. Only the final plague, the death of all firstborn sons, completely shook Pharaoh's illusion of power. We all have areas in our lives where we are a little like Pharaoh; we want to be in charge and make our own rules. But just as there is room for only one driver in a car, so there is room for only one God in your heart. Try to discern those areas in your life where you are still making the rules instead of living by God's rules—areas where you need to give up control to God. If you can root out pride before it begins to grow, you will save yourself much grief by avoiding God's judgment.

DIVINE PROMISE

WHAT SORROW FOR THOSE WHO ARE WISE IN THEIR OWN EYES AND THINK THEMSELVES SO CLEVER. *Isaiah 5:21*

Priorities

MY QUESTION *for* GOD

How can I focus on what is really important?

A MOMENT *with* GOD

Seek his will in all you do, and he will show you
which path to take.   PROVERBS 3:6

Wherever your treasure is, there the desires of your
heart will also be.   LUKE 12:34

As I looked at everything I had worked so hard to
accomplish, it was all so meaningless—like chasing
the wind. There was nothing really worthwhile
anywhere.   ECCLESIASTES 2:11

Martha was distracted by the big dinner she was
preparing. . . . But the Lord said to her, "My
dear Martha, you are worried and upset over all
these details! There is only one thing worth being
concerned about. Mary has discovered it, and it will
not be taken away from her."   LUKE 10:40-42

*I*magine that you're in the middle of a very personal
and significant conversation with a friend at the kitchen
table. Or that you're reading a Bible story to your
young daughter just before tucking her into bed. Then
the phone rings. What do you do? Most of us would
answer the phone, or at least check the caller ID. Why?
because interruptions tend to become top priorities.
Our lives seem to skip from one urgent interruption
to another. And all the while, we keep missing what is
really important. What are the things that matter most
in life, that are true priorities? How can we distinguish
true priorities from lesser ones, like the ringing phone?
The answer is this: Don't confuse what's urgent with

what's important. You must set your priorities first. Don't let everyone else decide what your day should look like—that should be between you and God. If you make God your first priority, he will give you the proper perspective on the rest of the activities in your day. Ask God to show you what is worth being concerned about.

DIVINE PROMISE

SEEK THE KINGDOM OF GOD ABOVE ALL ELSE, AND LIVE RIGHTEOUSLY, AND HE WILL GIVE YOU EVERYTHING YOU NEED. *Matthew 6:33*

Promises of God

MY QUESTION *for* GOD

What are some of the great promises of God?

A MOMENT *with* GOD

God loved the world so much that he gave his one and only Son, so that everyone who believes in him will not perish but have eternal life.   JOHN 3:16

The wages of sin is death, but the free gift of God is eternal life through Christ Jesus our Lord. ROMANS 6:23

God promises salvation to all who accept it. Those who believe that Jesus died for their sins, confess those

sins, and are truly sorry for them, will be saved from
the punishment their sins deserve. God looks at them
as if they had never sinned, and he gives them eternal
life in heaven.

If you love me, obey my commandments. And I
will ask the Father, and he will give you another
Advocate, who will never leave you. He is the Holy
Spirit, who leads into all truth.   JOHN 14:15-17

God promises to be with you forever in the form of
the Holy Spirit.

Teach these new disciples to obey all the commands
I have given you. And be sure of this: I am with you
always, even to the end of the age.   MATTHEW 28:20

God promises to be with you all the time.

If we confess our sins to him, he is faithful and just
to forgive us our sins and to cleanse us from all
wickedness.   1 JOHN 1:9

God promises to forgive you whenever you do wrong,
if you just ask him. He promises that nothing you do is
beyond his forgiveness.

Don't worry about anything; instead, pray about
everything. Tell God what you need, and thank him
for all he has done. Then you will experience God's

peace, which exceeds anything we can understand.
His peace will guard your hearts and minds as you
live in Christ Jesus.   PHILIPPIANS 4:6-7

*G*od promises you peace of heart and mind when you
entrust your life to him.

We know that God causes everything to work
together for the good of those who love God and are
called according to his purpose for them.   ROMANS 8:28

Our present troubles are small and won't last very
long. Yet they produce for us a glory that vastly
outweighs them and will last forever!   2 CORINTHIANS 4:17

*G*od promises to use even the bad things that happen
to you for good purposes.

The day of the Lord will come as unexpectedly
as a thief. Then the heavens will pass away with a
terrible noise, and the very elements themselves will
disappear in fire, and the earth and everything on it
will be found to deserve judgment.   2 PETER 3:10

*G*od promises that Jesus is coming back to judge the
world for its deeds.

Our dying bodies must be transformed into bodies
that will never die; our mortal bodies must be
transformed into immortal bodies.   1 CORINTHIANS 15:53

God promises that all who believe in him—living or dead—will be given new bodies that will never die.

Don't let your hearts be troubled. Trust in God, and trust also in me. There is more than enough room in my Father's home. If this were not so, would I have told you that I am going to prepare a place for you? When everything is ready, I will come and get you, so that you will always be with me where I am. And you know the way to where I am going." "No, we don't know, Lord," Thomas said. "We have no idea where you are going, so how can we know the way?" Jesus told him, "I am the way, the truth, and the life. No one can come to the Father except through me."

JOHN 14:1-6

God promises an eternal home in heaven for all who trust in Jesus Christ and acknowledge him as their Lord.

DIVINE PROMISE

DEEP IN YOUR HEARTS YOU KNOW THAT EVERY PROMISE OF THE LORD YOUR GOD HAS COME TRUE. NOT A SINGLE ONE HAS FAILED! *Joshua 23:14*

Provision

MY QUESTION *for* GOD

What does God provide for me?

A MOMENT *with* GOD

God will generously provide all you need. Then you
will always have everything you need and plenty
left over to share with others. As the Scriptures say,
"They share freely and give generously to the poor.
Their good deeds will be remembered forever."

2 CORINTHIANS 9:8-9

This same God who takes care of me will supply all
your needs from his glorious riches, which have been
given to us in Christ Jesus.   PHILIPPIANS 4:19

There's a big difference between wants and needs,
though we often have trouble making that distinction.
When you understand what you truly need and then
see how God provides it, you will realize how much
God cares for you. God doesn't promise to give you
a lot of possessions, but he does promise to help you
possess the qualities that reflect his nature so you can
accomplish his plan for you. He doesn't promise to pre-
serve your physical life, but he does promise to take
care of your soul for all eternity if you believe in him
and are committed to him.

Divine Promise

I WILL BE YOUR GOD THROUGHOUT YOUR
LIFETIME—UNTIL YOUR HAIR IS WHITE WITH
AGE. I MADE YOU, AND I WILL CARE FOR YOU.
I WILL CARRY YOU ALONG AND SAVE YOU.

Isaiah 46:4

Purpose

My Question *for* God

Does God have a specific purpose for my life?

A Moment *with* God

I cry out to God Most High, to God who will fulfill
his purpose for me.   PSALM 57:2

My life is worth nothing to me unless I use it for
finishing the work assigned me by the Lord Jesus—
the work of telling others the Good News.   ACTS 20:24

You didn't choose me. I chose you. I appointed you to
go and produce lasting fruit, so that the Father will
give you whatever you ask for, using my name.

JOHN 15:16

I take joy in doing your will, my God, for your
instructions are written on my heart.   PSALM 40:8

I press on to possess that perfection for which Christ
Jesus first possessed me.   PHILIPPIANS 3:12

*D*o you keep a to-do list of the things you need to accomplish each day, week, or month? Such lists can bring a sense of purpose to your life because they help you stay focused and on target. If you were to reduce your entire life's goals to a list of only three or four items, what would they be? The top item on that list should come close to identifying the purpose of your life. According to the Bible, your purpose is to be inspired with a vision of how God can best use you to accomplish his goals. God has both a general purpose and a specific purpose for you. In a general sense, you have been chosen by God to let the love of Jesus shine through you to make an impact on others. More specifically, God has given you unique spiritual gifts and wants you to use them to make a contribution within your sphere of influence. The more you fulfill your general purpose, the clearer your specific purpose will become. Your ultimate goal in life should not be to reach the destinations you want but to reach the destinations God wants for you. As you passionately pursue the purpose God has assigned you, God promises to give your life greater meaning, lasting significance, and eternal results.

DIVINE PROMISE

LET GOD TRANSFORM YOU INTO A NEW PERSON BY CHANGING THE WAY YOU THINK. THEN YOU WILL LEARN TO KNOW GOD'S WILL FOR YOU, WHICH IS GOOD AND PLEASING AND PERFECT.   *Romans 12:2*

Quitting

MY QUESTION *for* GOD

How do I know when it's time to quit or when I need to keep going?

A MOMENT *with* GOD

Think carefully about what is right, and stop sinning.

1 CORINTHIANS 15:34

Be strong and courageous, and do the work. Don't be afraid or discouraged, for the LORD God, my God, is with you. He will not fail you or forsake you. He will see to it that all the work . . . is finished correctly.

1 CHRONICLES 28:20

Do not let sin control the way you live; do not give in to sinful desires.   ROMANS 6:12

We are pressed on every side by troubles, but we are not crushed. We are perplexed, but not driven to despair. . . . We know that God, who raised the Lord Jesus, will also raise us with Jesus and present us to himself together with you. . . . That is why we never give up.   2 CORINTHIANS 4:8, 14-16

It is time to quit if you are doing something wrong, if you realize your actions are futile, or if you are hurting someone. Even if what you are doing is not inherently wrong, it may be time to quit if it is not productive, if it is absorbing too much of your time and attention, or if it is a stumbling block to others. However, when God has called you to a task, you should not give up. Not only will you miss out on the great blessing of reaching your goal, you might also experience God's discipline for not trusting him to help you get there. Just because God asks you to do something doesn't mean it will be easy. In fact, the more important the task, the harder it often is. If you know that God is in what you are doing or is taking you a certain direction, don't give up just because the going gets tough. If anything, that should tell you that you are headed in the right direction. Keep moving forward boldly in faith.

DIVINE ENCOURAGEMENT

LET'S NOT GET TIRED OF DOING WHAT IS GOOD. AT JUST THE RIGHT TIME WE WILL REAP A HARVEST OF BLESSING IF WE DON'T GIVE UP.
Galatians 6:9

Regrets

MY QUESTION *for* GOD

There are a lot of things in my past that I regret doing. How can I get over those regrets?

A MOMENT *with* GOD

Peter was sitting outside in the courtyard. A servant girl came over and said to him, "You were one of those with Jesus the Galilean." But Peter denied it in front of everyone. "I don't know what you're talking about," he said. Later, out by the gate, another servant girl noticed him and said to those standing around, "This man was with Jesus of Nazareth." Again Peter denied it, this time with an oath. "I don't even know the man," he said. A little later some of the other bystanders came over to Peter and said, "You must be one of them; we can tell by your Galilean accent." Peter swore, "A curse on me if I'm lying—I don't know the man!" And immediately the rooster crowed. Suddenly, Jesus' words flashed through Peter's mind: "Before the rooster crows, you will deny three times that you even know me." And he went away, weeping bitterly.   MATTHEW 26:69-75

I say to you that you are Peter (which means "rock"), and upon this rock I will build my church, and all the powers of hell will not conquer it.   MATTHEW 16:18

This means that anyone who belongs to Christ has become a new person. The old life is gone; a new life has begun!   2 CORINTHIANS 5.17

If the memories and experiences of your life were compared to rocks that you have collected and must carry around in a backpack, surely guilt and regret would be among the heaviest. Guilt is a legitimate spiritual response to sin. Regret is sorrow over the consequences of your decisions, both the sinful and the simply unfortunate. While God promises to remove your guilt when you seek his forgiveness, he does not prevent the consequences of your sin. It is likely the regret over those consequences that you are carrying, and it weighs you down with remorse. God promises to help you deal with your regrets so you can move on to the future without carrying a heavy load of guilt. When you come to faith in Jesus, he forgives your sins—all of them. He actually forgets your past, and he gives you a fresh start. You still have to live with the consequences of your actions because those cannot be retracted. But because God forgives and forgets, you can move forward without the heavy burden of regret. Because God no longer holds your past against you, you no longer need to hold it against yourself. You can be free from self-condemnation. Regrets can be so enslaving that they consume your thoughts and disable you from serving God in the future. If Peter had focused on the regret he experienced after denying Jesus, he would never have been able to preach the Good News so powerfully. Don't let regret paralyze you; let God's forgiveness motivate you toward positive action for him in the future. It is a divine moment when you truly grasp the power of God's healing forgiveness and are able to turn your regrets into resolve.

DIVINE PROMISE

DAVID ALSO SPOKE OF THIS WHEN HE DESCRIBED THE HAPPINESS OF THOSE WHO ARE DECLARED RIGHTEOUS WITHOUT WORKING FOR IT: "OH, WHAT JOY FOR THOSE WHOSE DISOBEDIENCE IS FORGIVEN, WHOSE SINS ARE PUT OUT OF SIGHT. YES, WHAT JOY FOR THOSE WHOSE RECORD THE LORD HAS CLEARED OF SIN." *Romans 4:6-8*

Relationships

MY QUESTION *for* GOD

Can a married man have close friendships with other women?

A MOMENT *with* GOD

Treat older women as you would your mother, and treat younger women with all purity as you would your own sisters.   1 TIMOTHY 5:2

Anyone who even looks at a woman with lust has already committed adultery with her in his heart.

MATTHEW 5:28

Let there be no sexual immorality, impurity, or greed among you. Such sins have no place among God's people. Obscene stories, foolish talk, and coarse jokes—these are not for you. Instead, let there be thankfulness to God. . . . So be careful how you live. Don't live like fools, but like those who are wise.

EPHESIANS 5:3-4, 15

Friendships with women are an important part of most men's lives, but they can also be a powerful source of temptation. Jesus had many female friends, some of whom supported his ministry and even traveled with him, so it is appropriate for men to have healthy friendships with women. However, married men must be extra cautious to ensure that any friendships with other women do not turn into emotional relationships in which strong feelings can become inappropriate intimacy. This betrays the trust and commitment a man shares with his wife. Here are three ways to safeguard yourself: Never be alone with a female friend; avoid talking about your marital problems; always treat other women with great respect. Doing these things will help you strengthen your relationship with your wife and with God.

DIVINE PROMISE

GOD BLESSES THOSE WHOSE HEARTS ARE PURE, FOR THEY WILL SEE GOD.   *Matthew 5:8*

Remembering

MY QUESTION *for* GOD

How can remembering help me in my walk with God?

A MOMENT *with* GOD

You must commit yourselves wholeheartedly to these commands that I am giving you today. Repeat them again and again to your children. Talk about them when you are at home and when you are on the road, when you are going to bed and when you are getting up. Tie them to your hands and wear them on your forehead as reminders. Write them on the doorposts of your house and on your gates.   DEUTERONOMY 6:6-9

O my people, listen to my instructions. Open your ears to what I am saying, for I will speak to you in a parable. I will teach you hidden lessons from our past—stories we have heard and known, stories our ancestors handed down to us. We will not hide these truths from our children; we will tell the next generation about the glorious deeds of the LORD, · about his power and his mighty wonders.   PSALM 78:1-4

When I see the rainbow in the clouds, I will remember the eternal covenant between God and every living creature on earth.   GENESIS 9:16

Remembering the past is an essential part of living in the present and the future. Life is a long journey; to live it to the fullest, you can't afford to forget some of the important lessons you've learned along the way. If you do forget, you're likely to repeat your mistakes. One way to remember important milestones and lessons of the past is to establish celebrations, anniversaries, or special times to pause and reflect on where you've been, who has helped you, and what God has done in your life. Try to remember the good and learn from the bad. Never forget what God has done for you. Talk about God's faithfulness—both in your life and in the lives of others—with your friends, family, children, and grandchildren so that you build a legacy of faith for future generations to remember.

DIVINE PROMISE

IF YOU LOOK CAREFULLY INTO THE PERFECT
LAW THAT SETS YOU FREE, AND IF YOU DO
WHAT IT SAYS AND DON'T FORGET WHAT
YOU HEARD, THEN GOD WILL BLESS YOU FOR
DOING IT.   *James 1:25*

Renewal

MY QUESTION *for* GOD

*My life is a mess; I just wish I could start all over again.
How can I experience renewal?*

A MOMENT *with* GOD

I will give you a new heart, and I will put a new spirit
in you. I will take out your stony, stubborn heart and
give you a tender, responsive heart.   EZEKIEL 36:26

"Come now, let's settle this," says the LORD. "Though
your sins are like scarlet, I will make them as white as
snow. Though they are red like crimson, I will make
them as white as wool."   ISAIAH 1:18

Throw off your old sinful nature and your former
way of life, which is corrupted by lust and deception.
Instead, let the Spirit renew your thoughts and
attitudes. Put on your new nature, created to be like
God—truly righteous and holy.   EPHESIANS 4:22-24

Create in me a clean heart, O God. Renew a loyal
spirit within me.   PSALM 51:10

*H*ow often we disappoint ourselves! We have such high hopes and pure intentions, but inevitably we find ourselves weary and burned-out with self-defeat, the burdens of everyday living, or the consequences of bad choices and sinful actions. The messiness of life can leave us feeling exhausted, not only physically but spiritually. So many of us are in desperate need of renewal. Renewal begins with God's compassion and a heart that is ready for change. When the two are brought together, renewal will happen. You will find a new beginning. Your soul will be refreshed, your life revived. God will restore any heart that seeks a new start. That new start begins when you turn to God and turn away from what has been bringing you down. Ask God to forgive your sin, which is working inside you to poison everything you do. Thank God that his forgiveness is not based on the magnitude of our sin but on the magnitude of his love. No sin is too great for God's complete and unconditional love. A heart that truly wants to change is a heart that is ready for the renewal that only God's Spirit can bring.

DIVINE PROMISE

THIS MEANS THAT ANYONE WHO BELONGS TO CHRIST HAS BECOME A NEW PERSON. THE OLD LIFE IS GONE; A NEW LIFE HAS BEGUN!

2 Corinthians 5:17

Repentance

MY QUESTIONS *for* GOD

What is repentance? What happens when I repent?

A MOMENT *with* GOD

There is forgiveness of sins for all who repent.

LUKE 24:47

Peter's words pierced their hearts, and they said to him and to the other apostles, "Brothers, what should we do?" Peter replied, "Each of you must repent of your sins and turn to God, and be baptized in the name of Jesus Christ for the forgiveness of your sins. Then you will receive the gift of the Holy Spirit."

ACTS 2:37-38

Repent of your sins and turn to God, so that your sins may be wiped away.

ACTS 3:19

If my people who are called by my name will humble themselves and pray and seek my face and turn from their wicked ways, I will hear from heaven and will forgive their sins and restore their land.

2 CHRONICLES 7:14

*H*ave you ever had the experience of driving in an un-familiar city and suddenly realizing that you were going the wrong way on a one-way street? What you do next is very much like the biblical idea of repentance—you make a U-turn and change your direction as fast as you can. Repentance is motivated by the realization that you have taken the wrong way in life. The Bible calls the wrong way sin. Repentance is admitting your sin and making a commitment, with God's help, to change the direction of your life. While repentance is not a popular concept these days, it is essential because it is the only way to arrive at your desired destination—heaven. Repentance makes change possible so you can experience God's fullest blessings, both now and for eternity. When you repent, it is a divine moment in which you decide to move toward God instead of away from him. Are you going in the right direction?

DIVINE PROMISE

COME BACK TO ME, AND I WILL HEAL YOUR WAYWARD HEARTS. *Jeremiah 3:22*

Reputation

MY QUESTIONS *for* GOD

Does God care about my reputation? Should I care about my reputation?

A MOMENT *with* GOD

Work willingly at whatever you do, as though you were working for the Lord rather than for people. Remember that the Lord will give you an inheritance as your reward, and that the Master you are serving is Christ. COLOSSIANS 3:23-24

Choose a good reputation over great riches; being
held in high esteem is better than silver or gold.

PROVERBS 22:1

The Holy Spirit produces this kind of fruit in our
lives: love, joy, peace, patience, kindness, goodness,
faithfulness, gentleness, and self-control.

GALATIANS 5:22-23

*P*eople often think that your personal life does not
matter as long as you perform well on the job or look
good in public. God, however, does not make a distinction between your public life and your private life. Justice, righteousness, integrity, mercy, honesty, fairness,
and faithfulness are essential traits of a godly person's
character and reputation because they reflect God's
character. That is why God cares about your reputation—and you should too. You will develop a good
reputation when you display the same godly integrity
in private as you do in public. What matters most is
not what others think of you but what God thinks of
you. This perspective helps you maintain consistency
between your public life and private life. Every time
you do something to please the Lord and enhance your
reputation with him, you will experience a divine moment in your relationship with God, and you will inspire trust in others.

DIVINE PROMISE

NEVER LET LOYALTY AND KINDNESS LEAVE
YOU! TIE THEM AROUND YOUR NECK AS A
REMINDER. WRITE THEM DEEP WITHIN YOUR
HEART. THEN YOU WILL FIND FAVOR WITH
BOTH GOD AND PEOPLE, AND YOU WILL EARN
A GOOD REPUTATION. *Proverbs 3:3-4*

Respect

MY QUESTION *for* GOD

How can I show respect to other people?

A MOMENT *with* GOD

Moses listened to his father-in-law's advice and
followed his suggestions.   EXODUS 18:24

Dear brothers and sisters, honor those who are your
leaders in the Lord's work. . . . Show them great
respect and wholehearted love because of their work.

1 THESSALONIANS 5:12-13

A despised Samaritan came along, and when he saw
the man, he felt compassion for him. Going over to
him, the Samaritan soothed his wounds.   LUKE 10:33-34

Joab bowed with his face to the ground in deep
respect and said, "At last I know that I have gained
your approval, my lord the king, for you have granted
me this request!"   2 SAMUEL 14:22

*E*very person has the need to feel respected. When David gave the order for Joab's plan be put into effect, Joab was overjoyed at the sense of his own worth. You can show respect to others in several ways: (1) Listen. Good listening gives dignity to others by putting them at the center of your attention. (2) Affirm. Saying "You're right" or "That's a good idea" is very powerful. (3) Act. Following through on other people's suggestions is the strongest possible statement of your respect for them. When it is necessary to disagree with others, you should do so with a respectful attitude. Implement these actions in your relationship with God as well. He deserves your greatest respect.

DIVINE PROMISE

BE CAREFUL TO LIVE PROPERLY AMONG YOUR UNBELIEVING NEIGHBORS. THEN EVEN IF THEY ACCUSE YOU OF DOING WRONG, THEY WILL SEE YOUR HONORABLE BEHAVIOR, AND THEY WILL GIVE HONOR TO GOD WHEN HE JUDGES THE WORLD. *1 Peter 2:12*

Responsibility

MY QUESTIONS *for* GOD

Am I really responsible for all of my actions? I can't help it when I do certain things.

A MOMENT *with* GOD

Do not let sin control the way you live; do not give in to sinful desires. Do not let any part of your body become an instrument of evil to serve sin. Instead, give yourselves completely to God, for you were dead, but now you have new life. So use your whole body as an instrument to do what is right for the glory of God. Sin is no longer your master, for you no longer live under the requirements of the law. Instead, you live under the freedom of God's grace.

ROMANS 6:12-14

When we think of a bad habit, we think of things such as smoking, drinking, and abusing drugs. But spreading gossip, complaining, and backbiting are bad habits too. Worry is a bad habit that can hurt you both physically and spiritually. One of Satan's great lies is that you are a victim who has no power to resist your impulses. The world teaches that heredity, environment, and circumstances excuse you from responsibility. In reality, everything you do is the result of a choice you make—and you are responsible for every choice. It's hard to resist every temptation and always make good choices. The good news is that God is more powerful than anything you feel controls you. When you tap into his power through prayer and the support of fellow believers, God breaks the chains that hold you and gives you the self-control to say no.

DIVINE PROMISE

**DON'T YOU REALIZE THAT YOU BECOME THE
SLAVE OF WHATEVER YOU CHOOSE TO OBEY?
YOU CAN BE A SLAVE TO SIN, WHICH LEADS TO
DEATH, OR YOU CAN CHOOSE TO OBEY GOD,
WHICH LEADS TO RIGHTEOUS LIVING.**

Romans 6:16

MY QUESTION *for* GOD

Why is rest important for me?

A MOMENT *with* GOD

The creation of the heavens and the earth and
everything in them was completed. On the seventh
day God had finished his work of creation, so he
rested from all his work. And God blessed the
seventh day and declared it holy, because it was the
day when he rested from all his work of creation.

GENESIS 2:1-3

It is a permanent sign of my covenant with the people
of Israel. For in six days the LORD made heaven and
earth, but on the seventh day he stopped working and
was refreshed.   EXODUS 31:17

The LORD is my shepherd; I have all that I need. He
lets me rest in green meadows; he leads me beside

peaceful streams. He renews my strength. He guides
me along right paths, bringing honor to his name.

PSALM 23:1-3

It is useless for you to work so hard from early
morning until late at night, anxiously working for
food to eat; for God gives rest to his loved ones.

PSALM 127:2

Our world of perpetual motion creates a world of
anxiety and stress. We take pride in telling each other
how busy we are, and we feel vaguely guilty if we stop
to relax. God did not intend for his people to live in
a state of frenzied activity. From God's own example in Genesis to the promises he makes in the New
Testament, it is clear that God wants us to have rest
and refreshment for our body and soul. Why would
the omnipotent God of the universe rest after doing
the work of creation? Surely it wasn't because the Almighty was tired! The answer is that God, in ceasing
from his work, proclaimed his rest to be holy. God
knew that we would need to cease from our work to
care for our physical and spiritual needs. Work is good,
but it must be balanced with regular rest and attention
to the health of your soul. Otherwise, you might miss
the divine moments God sends your way. Make sure
to carve out regular times for worship and spiritual
refreshment.

DIVINE PROMISE

COME TO ME, ALL OF YOU WHO ARE WEARY
AND CARRY HEAVY BURDENS, AND I WILL GIVE
YOU REST.   *Matthew 11:28*

Risk

MY QUESTION *for* GOD

Is there any risk associated with faith in God?

A MOMENT *with* GOD

When you work in a quarry, stones might fall and
crush you. When you chop wood, there is danger
with each stroke of your ax.   ECCLESIASTES 10:9

A prudent person foresees danger and takes
precautions. The simpleton goes blindly on and
suffers the consequences.   PROVERBS 22:3

Do not be afraid of the terrors of the night, nor the
arrow that flies in the day.   PSALM 91:5

Most of us try to minimize risk. We have insurance
policies, retirement accounts, and alarm systems. This
need to protect ourselves is not a bad thing unless it
keeps us from doing what we want to do, what we have
to do, or what we are called by God to do. The Bible
tells us that the Christian life is risky; spiritual growth
and success can only occur with some level of risk. Taking foolish chances is not the same as taking a risk—it's

either stupidity, or it's being totally unrealistic about your goals. Taking a risk entails having a worthy goal, a good chance of achieving it, and a strong dose of confidence. Risk-taking is necessary if you want to grow in your relationship with God. When he calls you to do something that is out of your comfort zone, obey him despite the risk of failing, and trust him to help you succeed. Though it may seem like a moment of risk, it will actually be a divine moment of growth.

DIVINE PROMISE

COMMIT EVERYTHING YOU DO TO THE LORD. TRUST HIM, AND HE WILL HELP YOU. *Psalm 37:5*

Romance

MY QUESTION *for* GOD

How can knowledge of romance affect my relationship with God?

A MOMENT *with* GOD

Like a lily among thistles is my darling among young women. . . . Like the finest apple tree in the orchard is my lover among other young men. I sit in his delightful shade and taste his delicious fruit.

SONG OF SONGS 2:2-3

Drink water from your own well—share your love only with your wife. Why spill the water of your

springs in the streets, having sex with just anyone?
You should reserve it for yourselves. Never share it
with strangers.   PROVERBS 5:15-17

I will win her back once again. I will lead her into
the desert and speak tenderly to her there. . . . I will
make you my wife forever, showing you righteousness
and justice, unfailing love and compassion. I will
be faithful to you and make you mine, and you will
finally know me as the LORD.

HOSEA 2:14, 19-20

*R*omance is the language of love that fosters intimacy
with another person. What a wonderful feeling when
someone expresses their affection for you, enjoys your
company, and is captivated by you! As you read the
Bible, you will discover that God himself is the origi-
nal romantic. He created the concept of intimate love
between husband and wife, and he loves a "happily ever
after" story. He also created an even deeper kind of
love—the love between Creator and the created. God
romances you in a way; he longs to have a deeper relationship with you, to be your God, to captivate you,
to give you joy and peace. He wants your relationship
with him to continue happily ever after, for all eternity.
Romantic love between a husband and a wife is a picture of this deeper love that God desires to share with
each person he has created. As you learn to romance
your wife, you will see more clearly the way God romances all his people, wooing them into a lifelong,
loyal, beautiful relationship with him.

DIVINE PROMISE

LONG AGO THE LORD SAID TO ISRAEL:
"I HAVE LOVED YOU, MY PEOPLE, WITH AN
EVERLASTING LOVE. WITH UNFAILING LOVE
I HAVE DRAWN YOU TO MYSELF." *Jeremiah 31:3*

Sacrifice

MY QUESTION *for* GOD

Why should I make a habit of sacrificing for the sake of others?

A MOMENT *with* GOD

Lay your hand on the animal's head, and the LORD
will accept its death in your place to purify you,
making you right with him.   LEVITICUS 1:4

This is real love—not that we loved God, but that he
loved us and sent his Son as a sacrifice to take away
our sins.   1 JOHN 4:10

He personally carried our sins in his body on the
cross so that we can be dead to sin and live for what is
right. By his wounds you are healed.   1 PETER 2:24

The law of Moses was unable to save us because of the
weakness of our sinful nature. So God did what the
law could not do. He sent his own Son in a body like
the bodies we sinners have. And in that body God
declared an end to sin's control over us by giving his
Son as a sacrifice for our sins.   ROMANS 8:3

Without the shedding of blood, there is no forgiveness.

                                              HEBREWS 9:22

A sacrifice is a kind of substitution. You give up one thing in order to obtain something of greater value. Parents may sacrifice a new car to save money for a child's education. A baseball player executes a "sacrifice bunt" to give a teammate an opportunity to score a run. In the Old Testament, a sacrifice was an act of worship in which the blood of an animal was shed as a substitute for the punishment the people deserved for their sins. They brought an animal to the altar, symbolically transferred their sins to it, and sacrificed it as their substitute. This allowed them to be pure and holy once again before God. It may seem like a strange and even barbaric ritual to us, but think how much worse it would have been if each person had to die for their own sins instead. Today we are desensitized to the seriousness of sin, but it is just as serious to God as it has always been. Sin separates us from God. God is holy; we are not. Holiness and sin cannot coexist. In Old Testament days, God provided a way for the sins of his people to be removed so they could be holy in his eyes. When Jesus died on the cross, he transferred the sins of all people for all time onto himself. No more sacrifices need to be made. Jesus was the final sacrifice. All you must do is recognize and confess your sin before God, then accept his gift of forgiveness. Whenever you make a sacrifice by giving something up for someone else, you can be reminded in some small way of God's sacrifice.

DIVINE PROMISE

JUST AS EACH PERSON IS DESTINED TO DIE
ONCE AND AFTER THAT COMES JUDGMENT, SO
ALSO CHRIST DIED ONCE FOR ALL TIME AS A
SACRIFICE TO TAKE AWAY THE SINS OF MANY
PEOPLE. HE WILL COME AGAIN, NOT TO DEAL
WITH OUR SINS, BUT TO BRING SALVATION TO
ALL WHO ARE EAGERLY WAITING FOR HIM.

Hebrews 9:27-28

Seeking God

MY QUESTION *for* GOD

*I feel like I'm still searching for God. How do I seek out a
relationship with him?*

A MOMENT *with* GOD

My heart has heard you say, "Come and talk with
me." And my heart responds, "LORD, I am coming."

PSALM 27:8

The LORD is close to all who call on him, yes, to all
who call on him in truth.   PSALM 145:18

Come close to God, and God will come close to you.

JAMES 4:8

When you have a close friend, you do your best to stay
in touch. You talk almost every day. You go out and do
things together, or you just reminisce with each other

about fond memories. It's no different with God. A relationship with God requires effort, activity, daily contact, and building memories. When you're seeking out a relationship with God, talk to him every day. Be open and honest, just as you would be with a close friend. Then take the time to listen. Allow a few moments each day for quality time with God. Express your concerns, talk about your future, or remember ways he's been with you and helped you in the past. Don't forget to ask him what he's doing, too, both around the world and in your life. Read his Word daily to open yourself up to what he might be saying to you. Remember that God is with you all day, every day. You can talk to him about everything that comes up at home, at work, and everywhere else. Share your thoughts, needs, and concerns with him as they arise. As you get to know God by spending time with him every day, you'll begin to find the relationship you desire. God promises that if you search for him, you will find him. You'll wonder how you ever got along without him.

DIVINE PROMISE
IF YOU SEEK HIM, YOU WILL FIND HIM.
1 Chronicles 28:9

Self-Control

MY QUESTION *for* GOD
Why do I always have to be thinking about self-control?

A Moment *with* God

I have discovered this principle of life—that when
I want to do what is right, I inevitably do what is
wrong. I love God's law with all my heart. But there
is another power within me that is at war with my
mind. This power makes me a slave to the sin that is
still within me. Oh, what a miserable person I am!
Who will free me from this life that is dominated by
sin and death? Thank God! The answer is in Jesus
Christ our Lord. So you see how it is: In my mind
I really want to obey God's law, but because of my
sinful nature I am a slave to sin.   ROMANS 7:21-25

Train yourself to be godly. Physical training is good,
but training for godliness is much better, promising
benefits in this life and in the life to come.

                                             1 TIMOTHY 4:7-8

Better to have self-control than to conquer a city.

                                             PROVERBS 16:32

Self-control is one of the hardest character traits to
maintain because it means denying what comes naturally to your sinful nature and replacing it with a godly
response. Developing self-control is a lifelong en-
deavor because just when you think you have one area
of your life mastered, another area gets out of control.
Sometimes it seems almost impossible to control your
thoughts, your words, and your physical appetites. But
self-control saves you from the consequences of giving in to sin and bad habits. Self-control begins with

God's work in you, but it requires your effort as well.
Just as a gifted musician or athlete must develop skills,
strength, and coordination through intentional effort,
striving for spiritual accomplishments must be intentional as well. God promises to reward your efforts.

DIVINE CHALLENGE

SUPPLEMENT YOUR FAITH WITH A GENEROUS
PROVISION OF MORAL EXCELLENCE, AND
MORAL EXCELLENCE WITH KNOWLEDGE, AND
KNOWLEDGE WITH SELF-CONTROL, AND
SELF-CONTROL WITH PATIENT ENDURANCE,
AND PATIENT ENDURANCE WITH GODLINESS.
2 Peter 1:5

Self-Esteem

MY QUESTION *for* GOD

How can I overcome my insecurities and be more confident?

A MOMENT *with* GOD

We are God's masterpiece. He has created us anew in
Christ Jesus, so we can do the good things he planned
for us long ago.   EPHESIANS 2:10

Not a single sparrow can fall to the ground without
your Father knowing it. . . . You are more valuable to
God than a whole flock of sparrows.   MATTHEW 10:29-31

Be honest in your evaluation of yourselves, measuring yourselves by the faith God has given us.   ROMANS 12:3

You should clothe yourselves instead with the beauty that comes from within, the unfading beauty of a gentle and quiet spirit, which is so precious to God.

1 PETER 3:4

To think more highly of yourself than you should is pride. But to think less of yourself than you should is false humility. And false humility can even turn into pride! Between the two extremes lies true self-esteem—an honest appraisal of your own worth. God values you highly because he loves you deeply. But you must not think you can be self-sufficient and live without God. Your sufficiency is in God. Your value is tied to the value he places on you and the purpose for which he created you. That makes you a man of great value indeed. If you struggle with insecurities, perhaps you are measuring your value by the wrong standards. The only thing that matters—and the only way to become confident—is to find your value as a creation and a masterpiece of God. When you understand how much God loves you, you will feel more confident in yourself. You should have a healthy self-esteem because with God you are capable of doing far more than you ever could have dreamed.

HOW PRECIOUS ARE YOUR THOUGHTS ABOUT ME, O GOD.   *Psalm 139:17*

Serving Others

MY QUESTION *for* GOD

Why is it important to serve others?

A MOMENT *with* GOD

I am the true grapevine. . . . Remain in me, and
I will remain in you. For a branch cannot produce
fruit if it is severed from the vine, and you cannot be
fruitful unless you remain in me. Yes, I am the vine;
you are the branches. Those who remain in me, and I
in them, will produce much fruit. For apart from me
you can do nothing.   JOHN 15:1, 4-5

You have been called to live in freedom, my brothers
and sisters. But don't use your freedom to satisfy your
sinful nature. Instead, use your freedom to serve one
another in love.   GALATIANS 5:13

Among you it will be different. Whoever wants to
be a leader among you must be your servant. . . . For
even the Son of Man came not to be served but to
serve others and to give his life as a ransom for many.

MATTHEW 20:26-28

A popular notion of success is being able to afford the luxury of having servants. Jesus turns this thinking on its head. He teaches that the highest goal in life is to be a servant. He places such a high value on serving because it is centered on others rather than yourself, and serving others is the essence of effective Christian living. When you are connected to Jesus, he turns your simple acts of service into something profound and purposeful. For example, he turns your simple act of singing into a profound chorus of praise that ministers to an entire congregation. He turns your simple act of tithing into a profound act of mercy that touches the heart of the needy person who benefits from it. He turns your simple act of teaching Sunday school into a profound moment in the heart of a child who suddenly realizes her need for salvation. He turns your simple act of visiting shut-ins into a divine moment of encouragement. When you step out in faith to serve others, God turns your simple acts into profound works for his Kingdom.

DIVINE PROMISE

ALL GLORY TO GOD, WHO IS ABLE, THROUGH HIS MIGHTY POWER AT WORK WITHIN US, TO ACCOMPLISH INFINITELY MORE THAN WE MIGHT ASK OR THINK. *Ephesians 3:20*

Sex

MY QUESTION *for* GOD

What does God think of sex?

A MOMENT *with* GOD

This explains why a man leaves his father and mother and is joined to his wife, and the two are united into one.
GENESIS 2:24

Because there is so much sexual immorality, each man should have his own wife, and each woman should have her own husband. The husband should fulfill his wife's sexual needs, and the wife should fulfill her husband's needs.
1 CORINTHIANS 7:2-3

Here is a strange thought—God likes sex! God created sex. He made men and women as sexual beings to procreate, to populate the next generation, and to express love and delight in each another. Think of it: He could have created us to reproduce by spores that float through the air, but instead he made sex a source of great enjoyment. God created sex for emotional and physical unity between a man and a woman in marriage. It is also a picture of the unity and intimacy a believer can have with God. Those who enjoy sex within the boundaries created by God will find fulfillment in their marriage, and they will better understand the importance of true intimacy with God.

Divine Promise

YOU CAN'T SAY THAT OUR BODIES WERE MADE
FOR SEXUAL IMMORALITY. THEY WERE MADE
FOR THE LORD, AND THE LORD CARES ABOUT
OUR BODIES.   *1 Corinthians 6:13*

Sin

My Questions *for* God

*Isn't sin kind of an outdated word? What exactly is
sin, anyway?*

A Moment *with* God

All have turned away; all have become useless. No
one does good, not a single one.   ROMANS 3:12

When you follow the desires of your sinful nature,
the results are very clear: sexual immorality,
impurity, lustful pleasures, idolatry, sorcery,
hostility, quarreling, jealousy, outbursts of anger,
selfish ambition, dissension, division, envy,
drunkenness.   GALATIANS 5:19-21

Remember, it is sin to know what you ought to do
and then not do it.   JAMES 4:17

The words you speak come from the heart—that's
what defiles you. For from the heart come evil
thoughts, murder, adultery, all sexual immorality,
theft, lying, and slander.   MATTHEW 15:18-19

Everyone has sinned; we all fall short of God's
glorious standard.   ROMANS 3:23

Sin will always be an offensive word. We can talk openly and impersonally about crimes like rape and murder; we can calculate statistics about adultery, unwed mothers, and divorce; we can trivialize greed, selfishness, and lust (or even raise them as cultural values)—but to call anything sin makes us uncomfortable. The word *sin* implies the violation of an objective, absolute standard of behavior established by God. We almost instinctively feel like this is an infringement on our rights. Yet that reaction displays a terrible misunderstanding of sin and an underestimation of God. When a doctor correctly diagnoses a disease in your body, you do not accuse him of impinging on your freedom; rather, you are grateful because he can treat the disease before it destroys your life. The Bible teaches that sin is a disease of the soul. It will destroy your life and lead to spiritual death if you do not treat it. God's standards of behavior are like preventative medicine; he prescribes them not to limit your freedom but to curtail the disease of sin. Not only is the antidote for sin free, but it also comes with the gift of eternal life.

DIVINE PROMISE

IF WE CONFESS OUR SINS TO HIM, HE IS FAITHFUL AND JUST TO FORGIVE US OUR SINS AND TO CLEANSE US FROM ALL WICKEDNESS.

1 John 1:9

Spiritual Dryness

My Question for God

Why can't I always maintain my enthusiasm for serving God?

A Moment with God

The seed on the rocky soil represents those who hear the message and immediately receive it with joy. But since they don't have deep roots, they don't last long. They fall away as soon as they have problems or are persecuted for believing God's word.   MATTHEW 13:20-21

You must warn each other every day, while it is still "today," so that none of you will be deceived by sin and hardened against God.   HEBREWS 3:13

Scorching temperatures, blazing sun, and too many days without rain will bring a drought. Plants wilt, streams dry up—everything is thirsty. You've probably experienced that parched feeling, when all you long for is a cup of cold water. Your soul can become dry, too, thirsting for something that will be truly fulfilling. Seasons of drought can come upon your soul when you experience the blazing pressures of life or the heat of temptation. Your desire to know God and serve him wilts and dries up. Just as a farmer must take extra care of his fields in a drought, so you must take care of your soul during times of spiritual dryness. Keep watering it with God's Word, and God will revive you with a sense of renewed purpose. Just as God sends the rain to refresh the earth, he also sends opportunities to revive your passion and purpose for him. When you see the chance to refresh your soul, act immediately to avoid unnecessary damage to your faith. When you get serious about your faith, your enthusiasm for God will grow by leaps and bounds. To protect your soul from the dangers of drought, read God's Word daily, study it, and refuse to be deceived by sin. Keep your focus on serving Jesus Christ. As you persevere, God will reward you with a divine moment of more joy than you ever thought possible.

DIVINE PROMISE

THE LORD WILL GUIDE YOU CONTINUALLY, GIVING YOU WATER WHEN YOU ARE DRY AND RESTORING YOUR STRENGTH. YOU WILL BE LIKE A WELL-WATERED GARDEN, LIKE AN EVER-FLOWING SPRING. *Isaiah 58:11*

Spiritual Gifts

MY QUESTION *for* GOD

How can I make myself more available for God's use?

A MOMENT *with* GOD

A spiritual gift is given to each of us so we can help each other. To one person the Spirit gives the ability to give wise advice; to another the same Spirit gives a message of special knowledge. The same Spirit gives great faith to another, and to someone else the one

Spirit gives the gift of healing. . . . In fact, some parts of the body that seem weakest and least important are actually the most necessary.   1 Corinthians 12:7-11, 22

God has given each of you a gift from his great variety of spiritual gifts. Use them well to serve one another.

1 Peter 4:10

I heard the Lord asking, "Whom should I send as a messenger to this people? Who will go for us?" I said, "Here I am. Send me."   Isaiah 6:8

Being available to God includes (1) the continual development of the gifts he has given you and (2) your willingness to use them to serve him in the calling he has given you. Do you know the unique gifts God has given you? If not, find out! Take a spiritual gifts assessment, or ask your friends what they think your gifts are. God gives each individual, including you, a spiritual gift and a special ministry in the church where you can use your gifts to help and encourage others and bring glory to his name. When you use your spiritual gifts, you help fulfill the purpose for which God made you. You can never use up these spiritual gifts; rather, the more you use them, the more they grow, allowing you to make a greater contribution within your sphere of influence. Using your spiritual gifts will give you plenty of divine moments when you find your greatest area of effectiveness for God and do your best work for him by helping others.

DIVINE PROMISE

THIS IS WHY I REMIND YOU TO FAN INTO
FLAMES THE SPIRITUAL GIFT GOD GAVE
YOU WHEN I LAID MY HANDS ON YOU. FOR
GOD HAS NOT GIVEN US A SPIRIT OF FEAR
AND TIMIDITY, BUT OF POWER, LOVE, AND
SELF-DISCIPLINE.   *2 Timothy 1:6-7*

Spiritual Warfare

MY QUESTION *for* GOD

*Are there really spiritual enemies or powers of darkness trying
to get me?*

A MOMENT *with* GOD

Then he said, "Don't be afraid, Daniel. Since the
first day you began to pray for understanding and
to humble yourself before your God, your request
has been heard in heaven. I have come in answer
to your prayer. But for twenty-one days the spirit
prince of the kingdom of Persia blocked my way.
Then Michael, one of the archangels, came to help
me, and I left him there with the spirit prince of the
kingdom of Persia."   DANIEL 10:12-13

Then Jesus was led by the Spirit into the wilderness
to be tempted there by the devil.   MATTHEW 4:1

*T*he Bible clearly teaches that human beings are involved in a spiritual battle. Rather than excluding

you from this warfare, your faith puts you right in the middle of it. You are in a battle for your very soul. You must recognize this reality so you can arm yourself, or else you will be overwhelmed.

We are not fighting against flesh-and-blood enemies, but against evil rulers and authorities of the unseen world, against mighty powers in this dark world, and against evil spirits in the heavenly places.

EPHESIANS 6:12

The enemy who planted the weeds among the wheat is the devil. MATTHEW 13:39

The world offers only a craving for physical pleasure, a craving for everything we see, and pride in our achievements and possessions. These are not from the Father, but are from this world. 1 JOHN 2:16

Satan is real and active, and his legions of demons are always on the attack. A battle rages in the spiritual realm. You can't see it, but you will experience if you seek to serve God. You need God's power in order to stand strong and resist temptation. Most of all, since you do not always know or understand the evil that is threatening you, you need God's power to give you strength to face the unknown. Have peace because God has already won the battle and uses his power to save you.

DIVINE PROMISE

THE LORD IS FAITHFUL; HE WILL STRENGTHEN YOU AND GUARD YOU FROM THE EVIL ONE.

2 Thessalonians 3:3

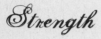

Strength

MY QUESTION *for* GOD

How can I experience God's strength in my life?

A MOMENT *with* GOD

I pray that from his glorious, unlimited resources
he will empower you with inner strength through
his Spirit. . . . Now all glory to God, who is able,
through his mighty power at work within us, to
accomplish infinitely more than we might ask
or think.   EPHESIANS 3:16, 20

The eyes of the LORD search the whole earth in order
to strengthen those whose hearts are fully committed
to him.   2 CHRONICLES 16:9

To keep me from becoming proud, I was given a
thorn in my flesh, a messenger from Satan to torment
me and keep me from becoming proud. Three
different times I begged the Lord to take it away.
Each time he said, "My grace is all you need. My
power works best in weakness." So now I am glad
to boast about my weaknesses, so that the power
of Christ can work through me. . . . For when I am
weak, then I am strong.   2 CORINTHIANS 12:7-10

A weight lifter's strength is measured by the number of pounds he can lift. A building's strength is measured by its resistance to external forces, such as wind or earthquakes. A corporation's strength is often measured according to its net assets. But how do you measure spiritual strength? The Bible teaches that spiritual strength is having the faith to move mountains, the power to lift burdens, a foundation deep enough to hold up against the forces of temptation, and the security of eternal salvation. How do you get this kind of strength? First, recognize that the power God used to raise Jesus from the dead is the same power that will raise you from the dead if you believe in him. And that same power is available to you now so you can live more effectively and courageously for him. Next, realize that God promises to give you inner strength through the power of his own Holy Spirit when you depend on him and trust him to do what is best for you. Finally, remember that God's power works best through your weaknesses. When you are weak and limited, God will supply the strength to help you overcome great obstacles. God loves to work through your weaknesses because then everyone can see that it is him, not you, supplying the strength.

DIVINE PROMISE

PHYSICAL TRAINING IS GOOD, BUT TRAINING FOR GODLINESS IS MUCH BETTER, PROMISING BENEFITS IN THIS LIFE AND IN THE LIFE TO COME. *1 Timothy 4:8*

Stubbornness

MY QUESTION *for* GOD

How do I know when I am stubborn?

A MOMENT *with* GOD

But no, my people wouldn't listen. Israel did not want
me around. So I let them follow their own stubborn
desires, living according to their own ideas.

PSALM 81:11-12

Pharaoh's heart, however, remained hard. He still
refused to listen, just as the LORD had predicted.

EXODUS 7:13

Be careful then, dear brothers and sisters. Make sure
that your own hearts are not evil and unbelieving,
turning you away from the living God. You must
warn each other every day, while it is still "today,"
so that none of you will be deceived by sin and
hardened against God. For if we are faithful to the
end, trusting God just as firmly as when we first
believed, we will share in all that belongs to Christ.

HEBREWS 3:12-14

You are stubborn when you refuse to believe that Jesus can make a difference in your life. You are stubborn
when you allow difficult circumstances to convince
you that God does not care; when you stop praying because you've made up your mind it won't help anyway;
when you refuse to trust God and instead depend on

your own strength. Do any of these situations describe you? At the core of stubbornness is the desire to disregard the overwhelming evidence against you. It is your way or no way. You just can't admit another way might be better, or worse yet, you don't even want to consider another option. The worst kind of stubbornness is when you refuse to consider that following God's rules for living, as found in the Bible, will make your life better. You've got your plans, and you don't want to admit that God's plan for your life might actually be better. You'd have to give up certain habits and lifestyle choices, and you just don't want to go there. Let God break through the stubbornness. He can show you how to give up those things you think are so good and exchange them for things he knows are so much better. When you humble yourself to admit there might be a better way, not only will you experience a divine moment with God, but you'll have a breakthrough in your relationships with others, too.

DIVINE PROMISE

I WILL GIVE YOU A NEW HEART, AND I WILL PUT A NEW SPIRIT IN YOU. I WILL TAKE OUT YOUR STONY, STUBBORN HEART AND GIVE YOU A TENDER, RESPONSIVE HEART. *Ezekiel 36:26*

Success

MY QUESTIONS *for* GOD

Is it okay to be successful in this life? How does God define success?

A MOMENT *with* GOD

All too quickly the message is crowded out by the worries of this life, the lure of wealth, and the desire for other things, so no fruit is produced.   MARK 4:19

Our goal is to please him. For we must all stand before Christ to be judged. We will each receive whatever we deserve for the good or evil we have done in this earthly body.   2 CORINTHIANS 5:9-10

Jesus replied, "You must love the Lord your God with all your heart, all your soul, and all your mind."

MATTHEW 22:37

Commit your actions to the LORD, and your plans will succeed.   PROVERBS 16:3

In this world success is usually defined by how much we own and how much we achieve. According to God's standards, success is measured not by material assets but by spiritual assets; not by what you have but by who you are; not by what you know but by who you know. Some people are successful both by the world's standards and by God's standards. There is nothing wrong with that, but it is also rare. We get into trouble when we gain material or worldly success at the expense of true success as God defines it. On the day of your death, you will lay aside all material assets; what you own here on earth has absolutely no eternal value. But how well you have succeeded in what God considers important counts in every way. Partnering with God in this life is the best way to ensure success in the next.

DIVINE PROMISE

STUDY THIS BOOK OF INSTRUCTION CONTINUALLY. MEDITATE ON IT DAY AND NIGHT SO YOU WILL BE SURE TO OBEY EVERYTHING WRITTEN IN IT. ONLY THEN WILL YOU PROSPER AND SUCCEED IN ALL YOU DO. THIS IS MY COMMAND—BE STRONG AND COURAGEOUS! DO NOT BE AFRAID OR DISCOURAGED. FOR THE LORD YOUR GOD IS WITH YOU WHEREVER YOU GO.   *Joshua 1:8-9*

Surrender

MY QUESTION *for* GOD

In the battles of life, when is it wise to surrender?

A MOMENT *with* GOD

Calling the crowd to join his disciples, [Jesus] said, "If any of you wants to be my follower, you must turn from your selfish ways, take up your cross, and follow me."   MARK 8:34

We died and were buried with Christ by baptism.
And just as Christ was raised from the dead by the
glorious power of the Father, now we also may live
new lives. . . . We know that our old sinful selves
were crucified with Christ so that sin might lose its
power in our lives. We are no longer slaves to sin.
. . . And since we died with Christ, we know we will
also live with him.   ROMANS 6:4-8

You cannot become my disciple without giving up
everything you own.   LUKE 14:33

Yes, everything else is worthless when compared
with the infinite value of knowing Christ Jesus my
Lord. For his sake I have discarded everything else,
counting it all as garbage, so that I could gain Christ.

PHILIPPIANS 3:8

*M*any of the greatest battles in history concluded
with surrender. One side realized they were powerless
against the other, and to save themselves they admitted
defeat and raised the white flag. In the spiritual realm
we fight two great battles, and surrender plays a part
in both. On the one hand, we fight against sin and its
control in our lives. If we are not allied with God, we
will surrender to sin and its deadly consequences. On
the other hand, we often foolishly fight against God and
his will for us because we want to have ultimate control
over our lives. This is the battle in which surrender is
necessary and positive. You surrender to God when
you finally realize that you are powerless to defeat sin

by yourself, and you give control of your life to God.
It is only when you have God on your side that you can
be victorious in your battle to defeat sin and pursue a
better life now and in eternity.

DIVINE PROMISE

THOSE WHO ARE DOMINATED BY THE SINFUL
NATURE THINK ABOUT SINFUL THINGS, BUT
THOSE WHO ARE CONTROLLED BY THE HOLY
SPIRIT THINK ABOUT THINGS THAT PLEASE
THE SPIRIT. SO LETTING YOUR SINFUL NATURE
CONTROL YOUR MIND LEADS TO DEATH. BUT
LETTING THE SPIRIT CONTROL YOUR MIND
LEADS TO LIFE AND PEACE.   *Romans 8:5-6*

Temptation

MY QUESTION *for* GOD

Why is temptation so dangerous?

A MOMENT *with* GOD

[Eve] saw that the tree was beautiful and its fruit
looked delicious. . . . So she took some of the fruit
and ate it.   GENESIS 3:6

Temptation comes from our own desires, which
entice us and drag us away.   JAMES 1:14

I am not surprised! Even Satan disguises himself as an
angel of light.   2 CORINTHIANS 11:14

*S*ome of Satan's favorite strategies are to make sin look desirable and good, and to convince you that what is really true is false. He knows exactly how to confuse you. He knows you well enough to take advantage of your weaknesses. In fact, Satan is even now taking aim at the places where you are most vulnerable. Don't let Satan trick you with lies. Arm yourself with the truth God gives you in his Word.

DIVINE PROMISE

KEEP WATCH AND PRAY, SO THAT YOU WILL NOT GIVE IN TO TEMPTATION. FOR THE SPIRIT IS WILLING, BUT THE BODY IS WEAK! *Matthew 26:41*

Temptation

MY QUESTION *for* GOD

Why do I give in to temptation?

A MOMENT *with* GOD

One day when Samson was in Timnah, one of the Philistine women caught his eye.   JUDGES 14:1

You have heard the commandment that says, "You must not commit adultery." But I say, anyone who even looks at a woman with lust has already committed adultery with her in his heart.

MATTHEW 5:27-28

Late one afternoon, after his midday rest, David got out of bed and was walking on the roof of the palace. As he looked out over the city, he noticed a woman of unusual beauty taking a bath. He sent someone to find out who she was.   2 SAMUEL 11:2-3

So guard your heart; do not be unfaithful to your wife.
                                                MALACHI 2:16

*W*hile Samson was in town, he noticed a beautiful woman. Temptation often begins with the eyes and travels quickly to the heart. What you do immediately after you see something or someone that poses a temptation for you will affect your thoughts and actions beyond the situation at hand. If you let your eyes linger where they shouldn't, your mind will follow and will find ways to justify your gaze. Then your heart will start tugging you in that direction. The first step in avoiding temptation is taking your eyes off whatever may be tempting you.

DIVINE PROMISE

THE TEMPTATIONS IN YOUR LIFE ARE NO DIFFERENT FROM WHAT OTHERS EXPERIENCE. AND GOD IS FAITHFUL. HE WILL NOT ALLOW THE TEMPTATION TO BE MORE THAN YOU CAN STAND. WHEN YOU ARE TEMPTED, HE WILL SHOW YOU A WAY OUT SO THAT YOU CAN ENDURE. *1 Corinthians 10:13*

Testing

MY QUESTION *for* GOD

Does God test the quality of my faith?

A MOMENT *with* GOD

Some time later, God tested Abraham's faith.

GENESIS 22:1

The LORD your God is testing you to see if you truly love him with all your heart and soul. DEUTERONOMY 13:3

We can rejoice, too, when we run into problems and trials, for we know that they help us develop endurance.

ROMANS 5:3

However, when ambassadors arrived from Babylon to ask about the remarkable events that had taken place in the land, God withdrew from Hezekiah in order to test him and to see what was really in his heart.

2 CHRONICLES 32:31

God blesses those who patiently endure testing and temptation. Afterward they will receive the crown of life that God has promised to those who love him. And remember, when you are being tempted, do not say, "God is tempting me." God is never tempted to do wrong, and he never tempts anyone else.

JAMES 1:12-13

Students are tested regularly to see if they are retaining and understanding the material they are learning. Auto consumers routinely take test drives to determine the quality of the vehicle they want to purchase. Companies invest vast sums in testing new products to guarantee they will perform as advertised. In the same way, our character and spiritual commitment are tested by the fires of hardship, persecution, and suffering. The Bible distinguishes between *temptation,* which Satan uses to lead us into sin, and *testing,* which God uses to purify us and move us toward spiritual growth and maturity. Out of testing comes a more committed faith. Just as commercial products are tested so that their performance can be strengthened, so also God tests your faith to strengthen you so you can accomplish all God wants you to do. When you feel like your faith is being tested, see it as a divine moment when God is working in your life to get your attention and to strengthen your relationship with him.

DIVINE PROMISE

DEAR BROTHERS AND SISTERS, WHEN TROUBLES COME YOUR WAY, CONSIDER IT AN OPPORTUNITY FOR GREAT JOY. FOR YOU KNOW THAT WHEN YOUR FAITH IS TESTED, YOUR ENDURANCE HAS A CHANCE TO GROW. SO LET IT GROW, FOR WHEN YOUR ENDURANCE IS FULLY DEVELOPED, YOU WILL BE PERFECT AND COMPLETE, NEEDING NOTHING. *James 1:2-4*

Thankfulness

My Question for God

Why should I give thanks to God?

A Moment with God

Give thanks to the LORD, for he is good! His faithful
love endures forever.   1 CHRONICLES 16:34

Give thanks to God because he is good, kind, and loving. Thanking God for these qualities helps you more
fully appreciate and respect them both in God and in
others.

He fell to the ground at Jesus' feet, thanking him for
what he had done.   LUKE 17:16

A thankful heart shows that your faith is maturing as
you recognize God's work in your life.

Thank God! He gives us victory over sin and death
through our Lord Jesus Christ.   1 CORINTHIANS 15:57

Thank God because he gives you victory over sin and
death when you put your faith in Jesus Christ.
Thank God for this gift too wonderful for words!

                                        2 CORINTHIANS 9:15

Thank God for the gift of his Son, Jesus, who paid the
price for your sin and calls you his friend.

Devote yourselves to prayer with an alert mind and a thankful heart.   COLOSSIANS 4:2

*T*hank God because he answers prayer. When you do, you acknowledge that God did something specific for you and that you are giving him the credit.

Since everything God created is good, we should not reject any of it but receive it with thanks.   1 TIMOTHY 4:4

*T*hank God for the goodness and beauty of creation.

Praise the LORD! I will thank the LORD with all my heart as I meet with his godly people. How amazing are the deeds of the LORD! All who delight in him should ponder them.   PSALM 111:1-2

*B*y giving thanks to God, you show others what he has done in your life and inspire them to pursue a relationship with him.

Even though the fig trees have no blossoms, and there are no grapes on the vines; even though the olive crop fails, and the fields lie empty and barren; even though the flocks die in the fields, and the cattle barns are empty, yet I will rejoice in the LORD! I will be joyful in the God of my salvation! The Sovereign LORD is my strength! He makes me as surefooted as a deer, able to tread upon the heights.   HABAKKUK 3:17-19

A spirit of gratitude and praise changes the way you look at life. Thankfulness and praise connect you to the source of real joy. When you make giving thanks a regular part of your life, you stay focused on everything God has done and continues to do for you. Expressing gratitude for God's help is a form of worship.

DIVINE PROMISE

IT IS GOOD TO GIVE THANKS TO THE LORD
. . . TO PROCLAIM YOUR UNFAILING LOVE
IN THE MORNING, YOUR FAITHFULNESS IN
THE EVENING.   *Psalm 92:1-2*

Thankfulness

MY QUESTION *for* GOD

How can I thank God when life is difficult?

A MOMENT *with* GOD

Joseph replied, "Don't be afraid of me. Am I God, that I can punish you? You intended to harm me, but God intended it all for good."   GENESIS 50:19-20

Be strong and courageous! Don't be afraid or discouraged because of the king of Assyria or his mighty army, for there is a power far greater on our side!   2 CHRONICLES 32:7

Be thankful in all circumstances, for this is God's will for you who belong to Christ Jesus.

1 THESSALONIANS 5:18

The difficulties of life come for many reasons. You may be experiencing the consequences of your own sin; you may be suffering because of someone else's sin; you may be caught in unfortunate circumstances that are really no one's fault. God may be testing your faith, or Satan may be targeting you to disrupt your godly influence on others and to discourage your faith. In any of these difficult circumstances, there are still reasons to thank God. He redeems your mistakes, teaches you wisdom through adversity, promises to help you through tough times, and guarantees you eternal life that is free from suffering. A God who redeems all troubles is a God worthy of praise and thanksgiving.

DIVINE PROMISE

HE WILL WIPE EVERY TEAR FROM THEIR EYES, AND THERE WILL BE NO MORE DEATH OR SORROW OR CRYING OR PAIN. ALL THESE THINGS ARE GONE FOREVER. *Revelation 21:4*

Thoughts

MY QUESTION *for* GOD

How can I stop dwelling on the bad thoughts that pop into my mind?

A Moment *with* God

It is what comes from inside that defiles you. . . . All
these vile things come from within; they are what
defile you.   MARK 7:20-23

Put me on trial, LORD, and cross-examine me. Test
my motives and my heart.   PSALM 26:2

Fix your thoughts on what is true, and honorable,
and right, and pure, and lovely, and admirable. Think
about things that are excellent and worthy of praise.

PHILIPPIANS 4:8

Controlling our thought life is perhaps one of the greatest struggles men face. God takes your thought life seriously because your thoughts disclose who you really are.
Even if you do not immediately act on your thoughts,
they do shape your attitudes and eventually your actions. A habit of dwelling on bad thoughts will eventually lead you to look for ways to act on those thoughts.
Temptation becomes too strong. You must allow God to
change the way you think by focusing your thoughts on
him and on anything that is true, honorable, right, pure,
lovely, admirable, excellent, and worthy of praise. You
can begin by reading Scripture, meditating on it, and
memorizing passages that focus on these good things.
When bad thoughts pop into your mind, immediately
redirect them to God's Word and ask God to change
your thought life. This takes great discipline but is very
effective. Each victory over negative thoughts is a divine
moment between you and God.

DIVINE PROMISE

I KNOW, MY GOD, THAT YOU EXAMINE OUR
HEARTS AND REJOICE WHEN YOU FIND
INTEGRITY THERE.   *1 Chronicles 29:17*

Time

MY QUESTION *for* GOD

How can I find the time I need?

A MOMENT *with* GOD

Teach us to realize the brevity of life, so that we may
grow in wisdom.   PSALM 90:12

Remember to observe the Sabbath day by keeping it
holy. You have six days each week for your ordinary
work, but the seventh day is a Sabbath day of rest
dedicated to the LORD your God. On that day no one
in your household may do any work. This includes
you, your sons and daughters, your male and female
servants, your livestock, and any foreigners living
among you. For in six days the LORD made the
heavens, the earth, the sea, and everything in them;
but on the seventh day he rested. That is why the
LORD blessed the Sabbath day and set it apart as holy.
                                                   EXODUS 20:8-11

He told them, "This is what the LORD commanded:
Tomorrow will be a day of complete rest, a holy
Sabbath day set apart for the LORD. So bake or boil
as much as you want today, and set aside what is left
for tomorrow."   EXODUS 16:23

Be careful how you live. Don't live like fools,
but like those who are wise. Make the most of
every opportunity in these evil days. Don't act
thoughtlessly, but understand what the Lord wants
you to do. Don't be drunk with wine, because
that will ruin your life. Instead, be filled with the
Holy Spirit.   EPHESIANS 5:15-18

Time is a lot like the life of a battery—we rarely know
how much is left until it's gone. With time, though,
we cannot buy more or borrow more from someone
else. That is why time is so valuable. Yet we often live
as though it means so little. All of us would admit that
we waste far too much time doing things that aren't important or significant. We let interruptions rule much
of our day. We know we should be more purposeful
about how we spend our time, but we're often unsure
about how to do that. The Bible is clear that how we use
our precious little time on earth will have an impact
on our life in heaven. We seem to live by the motto
"So much to do, so little time." But God does not ask
you to do *everything,* just everything he has called you
to do, and he assures you that there is enough time for
that. The more time you invest in discovering the purpose for which God created you and in living out that
purpose with obedience and responsibility, the more
meaningful and significant your time on earth will be.
The best way to find the time you need is to devote
time to God for worship and time to yourself for rest.
Devoting time to God gives you spiritual refreshment
and the opportunity to discover his priorities for you.

Devoting time to rest gives you physical refreshment and the energy to do what you are called to do in the time you have.

DIVINE PROMISE

FOR EVERYTHING THERE IS A SEASON, A TIME FOR EVERY ACTIVITY UNDER HEAVEN.... GOD HAS MADE EVERYTHING BEAUTIFUL FOR ITS OWN TIME. HE HAS PLANTED ETERNITY IN THE HUMAN HEART. *Ecclesiastes 3:1, 11*

Tired

MY QUESTION *for* GOD

What can I do when I'm tired but I have to keep going?

A MOMENT *with* GOD

Jacob's well was there; and Jesus, tired from the long walk, sat wearily beside the well about noontime.

JOHN 4:6

The Sovereign LORD is my strength! He makes me as surefooted as a deer, able to tread upon the heights.

HABAKKUK 3:19

Think of all the hostility he endured from sinful people; then you won't become weary and give up. . . . So take a new grip with your tired hands and strengthen your weak knees. HEBREWS 12:3, 12

Don't be afraid, for I am with you. Don't be
discouraged, for I am your God. I will strengthen you
and help you. I will hold you up with my victorious
right hand.   ISAIAH 41:10

Jesus said, "Come to me, all of you who are weary
and carry heavy burdens, and I will give you rest."
                                              MATTHEW 11:28

Be strong in the Lord and in his mighty power.
                                              EPHESIANS 6:10

𝒢od made us flesh-and-blood human beings. At creation, he set aside one full day of rest per week because
he knew we would need it. Jesus lived in a human body,
so he understands what it means to be tired. He understood the limitations of his disciples and led them
in taking regular breaks. Life is full and busy, but it
must be balanced by regular attention to the health of
your body and soul. Being overly tired is dangerous
because it can keep you from thinking clearly or cause
you to do or say something you'll regret. But when
it's impossible to get enough rest, your weariness is
an opportunity to experience God's faithfulness. He
will give you renewed strength when you grow weary.
When you come to him in praise, he refreshes your
heart. When you come to him in prayer, he refreshes
your soul. When you come to him in solitude, he refreshes your body. When you come to him in need, he
refreshes your mind. When you come to him in thankfulness, he refreshes your perspective. Coming to God

releases you from your burdens and allows you to draw strength from him, the source of strength.

DIVINE PROMISE

HE GIVES POWER TO THE WEAK AND STRENGTH TO THE POWERLESS. EVEN YOUTHS WILL BECOME WEAK AND TIRED, AND YOUNG MEN WILL FALL IN EXHAUSTION. BUT THOSE WHO TRUST IN THE LORD WILL FIND NEW STRENGTH. THEY WILL SOAR HIGH ON WINGS LIKE EAGLES. THEY WILL RUN AND NOT GROW WEARY. THEY WILL WALK AND NOT FAINT.

Isaiah 40:29-31

Tithing

MY QUESTION *for* GOD

I know I should tithe but I have so many other expenses. Is tithing really necessary in God's eyes?

A MOMENT *with* GOD

Honor the LORD with your wealth and with the best part of everything you produce.   PROVERBS 3:9

If it is giving, give generously.   ROMANS 12:8

You must each decide in your heart how much to give. And don't give reluctantly or in response to pressure. "For God loves a person who gives cheerfully."   2 CORINTHIANS 9:7

You should tithe.   MATTHEW 23:23

Give, and you will receive. Your gift will return to
you in full—pressed down, shaken together to make
room for more, running over, and poured into your
lap. The amount you give will determine the amount
you get back.   LUKE 6:38

𝒯ithing is not just a religious law. Tithing is both practical and symbolic. Practically, tithing is a means of
supporting the church and the work of believers around
the world. When we give, we do so because we believe
in the church and the work it is doing. Symbolically,
giving the first part of our earnings to the Lord demonstrates that he is our number one priority and that we
are grateful for the blessings he has given us. When we
tithe, not only are we supporting God's work, fellow
believers, and those in need, we are showing our commitment to God and honoring him for his provision and
faithfulness. A habit of tithing allows you to experience
a divine moment because it makes God your top priority and gives you the proper perspective on the rest of
your paycheck. Instead of asking, "How much of my
money do I need to give to God?" ask yourself, "How
much of God's money do I need to keep?"

DIVINE PROMISE

"YOU HAVE CHEATED ME OF THE TITHES AND
OFFERINGS DUE TO ME.... BRING ALL THE
TITHES INTO THE STOREHOUSE SO THERE WILL
BE ENOUGH FOOD IN MY TEMPLE. IF YOU DO,"
SAYS THE LORD OF HEAVEN'S ARMIES, "I WILL
OPEN THE WINDOWS OF HEAVEN FOR YOU.
I WILL POUR OUT A BLESSING SO GREAT YOU
WON'T HAVE ENOUGH ROOM TO TAKE IT IN!
TRY IT! PUT ME TO THE TEST!"   *Malachi 3:8-10*

Trust

MY QUESTION *for* GOD

What does it mean to trust God?

A MOMENT *with* GOD

You are worthy, O Lord our God, to receive glory
and honor and power. For you created all things.

REVELATION 4:11

*T*rusting God means recognizing that God is your
creator and knows what is best for you.

Christ will make his home in your hearts as you trust
in him. Your roots will grow down into God's love
and keep you strong.   EPHESIANS 3:17

*T*rusting God is an ongoing process that happens within a personal relationship with him.

"Build a large boat. . . . I am about to cover the earth with a flood." . . . Noah did everything exactly as God had commanded him.   GENESIS 6:14, 17, 22

*T*rusting God means obeying his commands even when you don't fully understand his reasons.

We are made right with God by placing our faith in Jesus Christ. And this is true for everyone who believes, no matter who we are.   ROMANS 3:22

*T*rusting God means depending on Jesus Christ alone for salvation.

Trust in the LORD with all your heart; do not depend on your own understanding. Seek his will in all you do, and he will show you which path to take. Don't be impressed with your own wisdom. Instead, fear the LORD and turn away from evil.   PROVERBS 3:5-7

*T*rusting God means acknowledging that he knows what is best and then surrendering to his plan.

You love him even though you have never seen him. Though you do not see him now, you trust him; and you rejoice with a glorious, inexpressible joy.

1 PETER 1:8

*T*rusting God requires faith.

Give all your worries and cares to God, for he cares about you.   1 PETER 5:7

*T*rusting God means that he has everything under control.

How joyful are those who fear the LORD and delight in obeying his commands.   PSALM 112:1

*T*rusting God means having the confidence that obeying him is the best way to live.

Though you do not see him now, you trust him; and you rejoice with a glorious, inexpressible joy.
                                                1 PETER 1:8

*T*rusting God means knowing he is there even though you can't see him.

DIVINE PROMISE

IF WE ARE FAITHFUL TO THE END, TRUSTING GOD JUST AS FIRMLY AS WHEN WE FIRST BELIEVED, WE WILL SHARE IN ALL THAT BELONGS TO CHRIST. *Hebrews 3:14*

Trust

MY QUESTION *for* GOD

Why is trust essential for strong relationships?

A MOMENT *with* GOD

Putting confidence in an unreliable person in times
of trouble is like chewing with a broken tooth or
walking on a lame foot.   PROVERBS 25:19

Who can find a virtuous and capable wife? She is
more precious than rubies. Her husband can trust
her, and she will greatly enrich his life. PROVERBS 31:10-11

The LORD detests double standards; he is not pleased
by dishonest scales.   PROVERBS 20:23

Distrust is unhealthy and painful in relationships because it causes you to question the motives of others.
Mutual trust strengthens and deepens relationships because you know that what others tell you is true and that
they are acting in your best interest. When you trust
someone, you have peace of mind about that person.
You are free to fully enjoy and engage in the relationship. Trust is vital in your relationships with your wife,
family, friends, neighbors, leaders, and coworkers. If
you can't trust someone, there is no way you can have
a healthy, close relationship. If you don't trust God,
the only One who is completely trustworthy, you cannot experience true peace or the ability to enjoy and
engage in a relationship with him. When you learn to

trust God, you will never have to question his motives or what he says. You will know that he always has your best interests in mind.

Divine Promise

THOSE WHO KNOW YOUR NAME TRUST IN YOU, FOR YOU, O LORD, DO NOT ABANDON THOSE WHO SEARCH FOR YOU. *Psalm 9:10*

Truth

My Questions *for* God

What is truth? Is anything really true anymore?

A Moment *with* God

In the beginning God created the heavens and the earth.   GENESIS 1:1

For you are God, O Sovereign LORD. Your words are truth.   2 SAMUEL 7:28

All Scripture is inspired by God and is useful to teach us what is true and to make us realize what is wrong in our lives. It corrects us when we are wrong and teaches us to do what is right.   2 TIMOTHY 3:16

The instructions of the LORD are perfect, reviving the soul. The decrees of the LORD are trustworthy, making wise the simple.   PSALM 19:7

Jesus responded, " . . . I was born and came into the world to testify to the truth. All who love the truth recognize that what I say is true."   JOHN 18:37

Jesus told him, "I am the way, the truth, and the life. No one can come to the Father except through me."

JOHN 14:6

Few things impact our daily lives as much as the concept of truth. First, there's "telling the truth." We gravitate toward those who tell the truth because they are honest and can be trusted. Without trust, relationships fall apart. We have to be truthful if we want relationships to work, companies to work, and government to work. Second, there's absolute truth. This includes the fundamental principles of nature, science, and human behavior that have been evident since the beginning of time. For example, the truth (or law) of gravity is that when you drop an object, it will fall. A truth of mathematics is that two plus two equals four. A truth of biology is that the right amounts of hydrogen and oxygen atoms make water molecules. A truth about life in general is that every person enters this world as a baby and someday exits this world through death. Only a fool would argue that these truths aren't valid. There is nothing any person can do to change these fundamental truths about how the world works. The Bible claims there is a third kind of truth: spiritual truth. This includes moral and supernatural principles about human relationships with God and others that are absolute and constant despite our feelings and beliefs to the contrary. Human beings have always wanted to determine this kind of truth for themselves or to believe it doesn't exist at all. While this kind of truth may be more difficult to accept and discover, it is the one that will most affect the way you live here on earth as well as your eternal destiny. Just as you can't reject the truth about gravity and expect to function well in this world, so you can't reject the truth about God and how he has determined life should work and expect your future to turn out the way you want it to. It's wise to discover and study this truth because it so completely impacts the life of every human being. You are free to ignore truth if you choose, but you do so at your own risk, both now and for eternity.

DIVINE PROMISE

TRUTHFUL WORDS STAND THE TEST OF TIME, BUT LIES ARE SOON EXPOSED. *Proverbs 12:19*

Truth

MY QUESTION *for* GOD

How can I tell whether something is true?

A MOMENT *with* GOD

Whatever is good and perfect comes down to us from God our Father, who created all the lights in the heavens. He never changes or casts a shifting shadow. He chose to give birth to us by giving us his true word. JAMES 1:17-18

God is not a man, so he does not lie. He is not
human, so he does not change his mind. Has he ever
spoken and failed to act? Has he ever promised and
not carried it through?   NUMBERS 23:19

*Y*ou only trust someone who is dependable, who can
always be counted on to tell the truth. God didn't just
create truth; he *is* truth. Therefore, God cannot lie.
You must believe that in order to believe this: Because
God cannot lie, everything he says in the Bible is true.
Keep reading through the Bible. Find God's promises
to you. Discover how much he loves you and wants a
close relationship with you. When you trust him with
your whole heart, he will make himself known to you
in amazing and powerful ways and you will experience
a breakthrough in your relationship with him.

DIVINE PROMISE

WE HAVE RECEIVED GOD'S SPIRIT (NOT
THE WORLD'S SPIRIT), SO WE CAN KNOW
THE WONDERFUL THINGS GOD HAS FREELY
GIVEN US.   *1 Corinthians 2:12*

Values

MY QUESTION *for* GOD

What is the benefit of having godly values?

A MOMENT *with* GOD

No one can serve two masters. For you will hate
one and love the other; you will be devoted to one
and despise the other. You cannot serve both God
and money.   MATTHEW 6:24

Wherever your treasure is, there the desires of your
heart will also be.   LUKE 12:34

Be on guard. Stand firm in the faith. Be courageous.
Be strong.   1 CORINTHIANS 16:13

These were his instructions to them: "You must
always act in the fear of the LORD, with faithfulness
and an undivided heart."   2 CHRONICLES 19:9

How do you spend your free time? What kind of en-
tertainment do you enjoy? Who are your best friends?
What do you think about most? How do you spend
your money? Your answers to these questions show
what your values are. Whatever you consider important, useful, and worthwhile is what you value. You
may have heard someone say, "He doesn't have any values." But such a statement is simply not true. Everyone
has values, either good or bad. The problem comes
when you don't have God's values but instead let the
world's values shape you. Your values are clear to those
around you because what you do, how you spend your
time and money, and what you talk about show exactly
what you value most. When you value God the most,
it will be reflected in the words you speak and how you
spend your time, energy, and money. When you love

and worship the Lord, obey him wholeheartedly, trust
him with your future, and serve him by serving others,
you are displaying godly values.

DIVINE PROMISE

WHO MAY WORSHIP IN YOUR SANCTUARY,
LORD? WHO MAY ENTER YOUR PRESENCE ON
YOUR HOLY HILL? THOSE WHO LEAD BLAMELESS
LIVES AND DO WHAT IS RIGHT, SPEAKING THE
TRUTH FROM SINCERE HEARTS.   *Psalm 15:1-2*

Victory

MY QUESTION *for* GOD

What does it mean to live the victorious Christian life?

A MOMENT *with* GOD

The temptations in your life are no different from
what others experience. And God is faithful. He will
not allow the temptation to be more than you can
stand. When you are tempted, he will show you a
way out so that you can endure.   1 CORINTHIANS 10:13

Put on every piece of God's armor so you will be able
to resist the enemy in the time of evil. Then after the
battle you will still be standing firm.   EPHESIANS 6:13

Pray in the Spirit at all times and on every occasion.
Stay alert and be persistent in your prayers for all
believers everywhere.   EPHESIANS 6:18

Every child of God defeats this evil world, and we achieve this victory through our faith. And who can win this battle against the world? Only those who believe that Jesus is the Son of God.   1 John 5:4-5

The Lord is a warrior; Yahweh is his name!

Exodus 15:3

Thank God! He gives us victory over sin and death through our Lord Jesus Christ.   1 Corinthians 15:57

*Y*our greatest victory has already been won by Christ, when you received God's gift of salvation. But you need daily victory over the strongholds of sin that threaten your ability to effectively live the Christian life. Sin destroys—sometimes dramatically, sometimes slowly. Sin harasses you, constantly threatening to draw you away from your relationship with God. To live a victorious life, you must relentlessly battle against sin and remove it from your heart piece by piece. When you trust Jesus Christ with your life, he equips you with everything you need to conquer sin and gain the victory.

Divine Promise

THEY WILL FIGHT AGAINST YOU LIKE AN ATTACKING ARMY, BUT I WILL MAKE YOU AS SECURE AS A FORTIFIED WALL OF BRONZE. THEY WILL NOT CONQUER YOU, FOR I AM WITH YOU TO PROTECT AND RESCUE YOU. I, THE LORD, HAVE SPOKEN! *Jeremiah 15:20*

Vision

MY QUESTION *for* GOD

How do I get a better vision of what I should be doing for God?

A MOMENT *with* GOD

It was by faith that Moses left the land of Egypt,
not fearing the king's anger. He kept right on going
because he kept his eyes on the one who is invisible.

HEBREWS 11:27

[Jesus said,] "I tell you the truth, anyone who believes
in me will do the same works I have done, and
even greater works, because I am going to be with
the Father."   JOHN 14:12

Don't copy the behavior and customs of this world,
but let God transform you into a new person by
changing the way you think. Then you will learn to
know God's will for you, which is good and pleasing
and perfect.   ROMANS 12:2

The LORD directs our steps, so why try to
understand everything along the way?   PROVERBS 20:24

Open my eyes to see.   PSALM.119:18

It's been said, "Vision is a picture of the future that
produces a passion in the present." If you lack vision,
it's like trying to see underwater without a mask—everything is blurry, nothing makes sense, and you feel
impossibly lost. If you want to have purpose, if you

want to clearly see your way in life, if you want to be motivated to do something that counts, you need vision—a picture of where you want to be at some point in the future. Having spiritual vision is having God's picture of your future. How do you capture God's vision of where he wants you to be and what he created you to accomplish? It's only when you empty yourself of your own opinions and dreams of the future that God can fill you with his vision. Here are several ways to fill yourself with God's vision for your life: through the study of his Word, through the conscience he has given you, through the counsel of other believers, and through prayer. Ironically, the only way that many of us can see better with our eyes is to get corrective lenses. To have better spiritual vision, you need the lens of faith—the ability to believe that there is more to life than what you see, that God is at work and has a place for you in his plan. As you learn to see through the lens of faith, God's vision for you will become clear.

DIVINE PROMISE

NOW ALL GLORY TO GOD, WHO IS ABLE, THROUGH HIS MIGHTY POWER AT WORK WITHIN US, TO ACCOMPLISH INFINITELY MORE THAN WE MIGHT ASK OR THINK. *Ephesians 3:20*

Vulnerability

I don't like being vulnerable with other people. Do I need to be?

The LORD sees clearly what a man does, examining every path he takes.   PROVERBS 5:21

The word of God is alive and powerful. It is sharper than the sharpest two-edged sword, cutting between soul and spirit, between joint and marrow. It exposes our innermost thoughts and desires. Nothing in all creation is hidden from God. Everything is naked and exposed before his eyes, and he is the one to whom we are accountable.   HEBREWS 4:12-13

Search me, O God, and know my heart; test me and know my anxious thoughts. Point out anything in me that offends you, and lead me along the path of everlasting life.   PSALM 139:23-24

What if others knew who you really are, deep down inside? Is there anyone with whom you can share your deepest fears, hurts, or doubts? The Bible teaches that every human being has a need for intimate relationships, but you are to choose carefully to whom you reveal your heart. Vulnerability occurs in only the most intimate relationships because it requires you to reveal your fears, hurts, doubts, and the darkest things in your life, the things you never want to come out in the open. You probably resist being vulnerable with God about your sins, especially the ones you don't want to give up. But vulnerability requires full disclosure, not hiding or covering up. It is only through vulnerability that we find true healing, restoration, renewal, and forgiveness. It is only through vulnerability that you can experience a breakthrough in your relationship with God. When you confess your sin, seek forgiveness, and commit yourself to following God's ways, your relationship with God and with others will be restored; a great weight will be lifted from you. While you cannot—and should not—be vulnerable with everyone, you can and should trust God, as well as a few others, to handle your deepest feelings with care. Vulnerability is the key to having divine moments in your most important relationships.

Divine Promise
IF WE CONFESS OUR SINS TO HIM, HE IS FAITHFUL AND JUST TO FORGIVE US OUR SINS AND TO CLEANSE US FROM ALL WICKEDNESS.
1 John 1:9

Waiting

My Question *for* God
How can waiting make my faith stronger?

A MOMENT *with* GOD

The LORD your God will drive those nations out
ahead of you little by little. You will not clear them
away all at once, otherwise the wild animals would
multiply too quickly for you.   DEUTERONOMY 7:22

There is so much more I want to tell you, but you
can't bear it now.   JOHN 16:12

When the right time came, God sent his Son.

GALATIANS 4:4

God often asks you to wait while leading you along
the path of progressive rather than immediate results.
Why? Sometimes waiting keeps you from the pride
that often comes after success. Sometimes it saves you
from defeat. And sometimes God makes you wait to
prepare you for a special task he has for you. God never
sees waiting as wasted time, so don't waste it by being
anxious. Serve God as you wait for him to accomplish
the next good thing in your life.

DIVINE PROMISE

BE STILL IN THE PRESENCE OF THE LORD, AND
WAIT PATIENTLY FOR HIM TO ACT. DON'T
WORRY ABOUT EVIL PEOPLE WHO PROSPER OR
FRET ABOUT THEIR WICKED SCHEMES. *Psalm 37:7*

Warnings

MY QUESTION *for* GOD

How should I view God's warnings?

A MOMENT *with* GOD

You must warn each other every day, while it is still "today," so that none of you will be deceived by sin and hardened against God. . . . Remember what it says: "Today when you hear his voice, don't harden your hearts as Israel did when they rebelled."

HEBREWS 3:13-15

The laws of the LORD are true; each one is fair. They are more desirable than gold, even the finest gold. They are sweeter than honey, even honey dripping from the comb. They are a warning to your servant, a great reward for those who obey them.   PSALM 19:9-11

To whom can I give warning? Who will listen when I speak? Their ears are closed, and they cannot hear. They scorn the word of the LORD. They don't want to listen at all.   JEREMIAH 6:10

Our society is full of warnings. A red light at an intersection warns you to stop. A poison label warns you to put that product out of the reach of children. An ambulance siren warns you to get out of the way. How you view these warnings is a matter of perspective. You can look at them as intrusions that prevent you from enjoying life, or you can look at them as blessings that protect you so you can enjoy life more. God's warnings are designed to protect his people from the consequences of foolish actions. For example, God's warning to avoid sexual immorality prevents you from the possibility of a broken heart, an unplanned pregnancy, or a sexually transmitted disease. All too often we view these warnings as obstacles to our freedom. When we do that, we rebel against the very things that are designed to protect us. God's warnings are his way of trying to save you from doing something you'll later regret.

DIVINE PROMISE

IF YOU LISTEN TO THESE COMMANDS OF THE LORD YOUR GOD THAT I AM GIVING YOU TODAY, AND IF YOU CAREFULLY OBEY THEM, THE LORD WILL MAKE YOU THE HEAD AND NOT THE TAIL, AND YOU WILL ALWAYS BE ON TOP AND NEVER AT THE BOTTOM. *Deuteronomy 28:13*

Will of God

MY QUESTION *for* GOD

What is God's will for my life?

A MOMENT *with* GOD

Who knows if perhaps you were made queen for just such a time as this?   ESTHER 4:14

You see me when I travel and when I rest at home. You know everything I do.   PSALM 139:3

"For I know the plans I have for you," says the LORD. "They are plans for good and not for disaster, to give you a future and a hope."   JEREMIAH 29:11

Come, let us go up to the mountain of the LORD, to the house of Jacob's God. There he will teach us his ways, and we will walk in his paths.   ISAIAH 2:3

Well done, my good and faithful servant. You have been faithful in handling this small amount, so now I will give you many more responsibilities.

MATTHEW 25:21

Oh, that we might know the LORD! Let us press on to know him. He will respond to us.   HOSEA 6:3

"So why do you keep calling me 'Lord, Lord!' when you don't do what I say? I will show you what it's like when someone comes to me, listens to my teaching, and then follows it."   LUKE 6:46-47

*H*as there ever been a Christian who has not asked this question? Sometimes "God's will" seems so vague, so hard to know. Perhaps the problem is that too often we're expecting God to reveal something special to us and we ignore the revelation he's already given in his Word. The Bible has dozens of clear commands for you to follow: Worship only God, love your neighbors and your enemies, use your spiritual gifts, tell the truth, do not covet, do not steal, be sexually pure, remain faithful, teach your children spiritual truths, don't gossip, be generous, don't take God's name in vain, read his

Word regularly, don't let money control you, let the Holy Spirit control your life—the list goes on! Isn't doing all these things God's will for your life? But God also created each person for a specific purpose, and he calls you to do specific tasks. It is usually through steady obedience to the will in his Word that your specific direction in life can be found. So first make sure you are following God's will in the areas he has already laid out. As you wait for God to reveal what he wants you to do specifically, you should continue to be obedient to the things he calls every person to do. Then, if you happen to miss God's direction for a specific task, you won't have missed God's will for living your everyday life. God is vitally interested in the details of your life, but his primary will for all people is simply obedience.

DIVINE PROMISE

THE LORD SAYS, "I WILL GUIDE YOU ALONG THE BEST PATHWAY FOR YOUR LIFE. I WILL ADVISE YOU AND WATCH OVER YOU." *Psalm 32:8*

Wisdom

MY QUESTION *for* GOD

How can I gain more wisdom?

A MOMENT *with* GOD

Fear of the LORD is the foundation of wisdom.
Knowledge of the Holy One results in good judgment.

PROVERBS 9:10

Give me an understanding heart so that I can govern
your people well and know the difference between
right and wrong.

1 KINGS 3:9

My child, don't lose sight of common sense and
discernment. Hang on to them, for they will refresh
your soul. They are like jewels on a necklace. They
keep you safe on your way, and your feet will not
stumble. You can go to bed without fear; you will lie
down and sleep soundly. . . . For the LORD is your
security. He will keep your foot from being caught
in a trap.

PROVERBS 3:21-26

Using a dull ax requires great strength, so sharpen
the blade. That's the value of wisdom; it helps
you succeed.

ECCLESIASTES 10:10

If you need wisdom, ask our generous God, and he
will give it to you. He will not rebuke you for asking.

JAMES 1:5

Solving a complex problem in trigonometry or writing a computer program that will guide a nuclear mis-
sile both require great intelligence. But intelligence
does not guarantee a balanced, productive, or fulfilling life. On the other hand, success in relationships,
raising godly children, and reaching spiritual maturity

depend more on wisdom than intelligence. The Bible has so much to say about wisdom (the entire book of Proverbs is devoted to it) because successfully navigating through life requires so much of it. Wisdom helps you recognize that an all-powerful, all-knowing God has designed a moral universe in which there are consequences for your choices, either good or bad. Wisdom begins with understanding your accountability to your Creator and your full dependence on him. It's not *what* you know but *who* you know. Wisdom from God helps you develop a godly perspective that penetrates the deceptive and distorted messages of this world. Wisdom is choosing to apply God's truth and principles to your daily relationships and situations. It helps you know the difference between good and bad, right and wrong.

DIVINE PROMISE

THE WISE ARE MIGHTIER THAN THE STRONG,
AND THOSE WITH KNOWLEDGE GROW
STRONGER AND STRONGER.   *Proverbs 24:5*

Words

MY QUESTION *for* GOD

Do my words matter as much as my actions?

A MOMENT *with* GOD

If you claim to be religious but don't control your tongue, you are fooling yourself, and your religion is worthless. JAMES 1:26

Who may worship in your sanctuary, LORD? Who may enter your presence on your holy hill? Those who lead blameless lives and do what is right, speaking the truth from sincere hearts. Those who refuse to gossip or harm their neighbors or speak evil of their friends. PSALM 15:1-3

I tell you this, you must give an account on judgment day for every idle word you speak. The words you say will either acquit you or condemn you.

MATTHEW 12:36-37

Let everything you say be good and helpful, so that your words will be an encouragement to those who hear them. EPHESIANS 4:29

The words you speak come from the heart—that's what defiles you. For from the heart come evil thoughts, murder, adultery, all sexual immorality, theft, lying, and slander. MATTHEW 15:18-19

May the words of my mouth and the meditation of my heart be pleasing to you, O LORD, my rock and my redeemer. PSALM 19:14

*O*ur words are like gifts that we give to God or to other people. The things we say and the meaning behind our words have an enormous impact on those who hear them. You wouldn't give an obscene gift to the president of your company, or even to a friend, and you certainly wouldn't want to give something insulting to an enemy. Words are no different. In fact, the greatest gift you can give to others is not in a box covered with paper and bows but in the words you use to encourage, inspire, comfort, and challenge them. Don't let your words be annoying, insulting, demeaning, or simply useless. Your words truly matter because what you say reveals the condition of your heart. Perhaps more than anything else, your words have the power to bring a divine moment to others.

DIVINE PROMISE

THE WORDS OF THE GODLY ARE A LIFE-GIVING FOUNTAIN. *Proverbs 10:11*

Work

MY QUESTION *for* GOD

How do I find meaning in my work?

A MOMENT *with* GOD

Make it your goal to live a quiet life, minding your own business and working with your hands, just as we instructed you before. Then people who are not Christians will respect the way you live, and you will not need to depend on others.   1 THESSALONIANS 4:11-12

Whatever you do or say, do it as a representative of
the Lord Jesus, giving thanks through him to God
the Father.   COLOSSIANS 3:17

You know that these hands of mine have worked to
supply my own needs and even the needs of those
who were with me. And I have been a constant
example of how you can help those in need by
working hard.   ACTS 20:34-35

Work with enthusiasm, as though you were working
for the Lord rather than for people.   EPHESIANS 6:7

Work is part of God's plan for our lives, so our work
matters to God. Those who work diligently experience many benefits in their own lives and are able to
pass them on to others. At its best, work honors God
and brings meaning and joy to your life. In your work
you should model characteristics of God's work, such
as excellence, concern for the well-being of others,
purpose, beauty, and service. When you have the perspective that you are actually working for God, you
can focus less on the task itself and more on your motives—to help people know God. The excitement and
interest that come from having this perspective are not
primarily from your work but from the One for whom
you work. God promises two basic rewards for faithful
work, regardless of the job: You are a more credible
witness to unbelievers, and your needs are met without
having to depend on others financially. Whatever your
job, there is immense dignity in all honest human labor
because your work is an opportunity to serve God and

others. Believe that God has placed you in your position for a reason, and then do your work well until he opens a door of opportunity for you to move on.

DIVINE PROMISE

WORK WILLINGLY AT WHATEVER YOU DO, AS THOUGH YOU WERE WORKING FOR THE LORD RATHER THAN FOR PEOPLE. REMEMBER THAT THE LORD WILL GIVE YOU AN INHERITANCE AS YOUR REWARD, AND THAT THE MASTER YOU ARE SERVING IS CHRIST.   *Colossians 3:23-24*

Worry

MY QUESTION *for* GOD

What can I do when worry overwhelms me?

A MOMENT *with* GOD

Don't worry about tomorrow, for tomorrow will bring its own worries. Today's trouble is enough for today.   MATTHEW 6:34

Here on earth you will have many trials and sorrows. But take heart, because I have overcome the world."

JOHN 16:33

Worry is a misuse of your God-given imagination. Most of the things you worry about will never actually happen, so you end up wasting your time and energy for nothing.

When you feel consumed by worry, make the conscious effort to turn your thoughts into a prayer. Tell your concerns to God, and turn them over to him. There is no problem that God cannot overcome. Because you have God taking care of you, you have no need to worry.

DIVINE PROMISE

THE LORD KEEPS WATCH OVER YOU AS YOU COME AND GO, BOTH NOW AND FOREVER.
Psalm 121:8

Worship

MY QUESTION *for* GOD

How should I worship God?

A MOMENT *with* GOD

David praised the LORD in the presence of the whole assembly: "O LORD, the God of our ancestor Israel, may you be praised forever and ever! Yours, O LORD, is the greatness, the power, the glory, the victory, and the majesty. Everything in the heavens and on earth is yours, O LORD, and this is your kingdom. We adore you as the one who is over all things. Wealth and honor come from you alone, for you rule over everything. Power and might are in your hand, and at your discretion people are made great and given strength. O our God, we thank you and praise your glorious name!"   1 CHRONICLES 29:10-13

Oh, how great are God's riches and wisdom and knowledge! How impossible it is for us to understand his decisions and his ways! For who can know the Lord's thoughts? Who knows enough to give him advice? And who has given him so much that he needs to pay it back? For everything comes from him and exists by his power and is intended for his glory. All glory to him forever! Amen.   ROMANS 11:33-36

We do not think of our world as a worshiping culture, let alone an idolatrous culture, but our behavior suggests otherwise. Consider our weekly gatherings of thousands of frenzied fans observing a ceremony of men dressed in strange garb acting out a violent drama of conquest. Others stay at home and join in by way of a small glowing shrine set up in the family room. Fans of professional football are probably not even aware that their behavior could be described as worship. Human beings were created to worship. To worship is to ascribe ultimate value to an object, person, or God, and then to revere, adore, pay homage to, and obey by ordering the priorities of our lives around whatever it is we worship. The Bible teaches that God alone is worthy of our worship. True worship, then, is the recognition of who God is and of who you are in relation to him. Ultimately, everything you do should be based on what you think of the almighty God and how you worship him. If you aren't giving honor to God, then you are worshiping someone or something else. More than anything else, worship will connect you with God, your only source of lasting hope and joy.

DIVINE PROMISE

THEREFORE, GOD ELEVATED HIM TO THE PLACE
OF HIGHEST HONOR AND GAVE HIM THE NAME
ABOVE ALL OTHER NAMES, THAT AT THE NAME
OF JESUS EVERY KNEE SHOULD BOW, IN HEAVEN
AND ON EARTH AND UNDER THE EARTH, AND
EVERY TONGUE CONFESS THAT JESUS CHRIST IS
LORD, TO THE GLORY OF GOD THE FATHER.

Philippians 2:9-11

Worth

MY QUESTIONS *for* GOD

What is my worth? What is my value to God?

A MOMENT *with* GOD

God created human beings in his own image. In the
image of God he created them; male and female he
created them.   GENESIS 1:27

You made [people] only a little lower than God and
crowned them with glory and honor.   PSALM 8:5

The LORD has declared today that you are his people,
his own special treasure, just as he promised, and that
you must obey all his commands.   DEUTERONOMY 26:18

Even before he made the world, God loved us and
chose us in Christ to be holy and without fault in his
eyes. God decided in advance to adopt us into his
own family by bringing us to himself through Jesus
Christ. This is what he wanted to do, and it gave him

great pleasure. So we praise God for the glorious
grace he has poured out on us who belong to his
dear Son. He is so rich in kindness and grace that he
purchased our freedom with the blood of his Son and
forgave our sins.   EPHESIANS 1:4-7

*D*o you get your sense of self-worth from a combina-
tion of looks, accomplishments, career, possessions,
and social status? This is a precarious way to live.
When you age or become ill, if your next performance
doesn't exceed your last, if you lose your job or retire,
if you meet with ill fortune and see your assets disappear, or if your friends are shallow and fickle—then
you also lose your sense of self-worth. The most secure
and lasting place to find worth is in your relationship
with God. It is truly a divine moment when you realize
just how much God values you! God created you and
knew you intimately before you were born. He loved
you enough to rescue you from eternal punishment for
your sins through Jesus' death and resurrection. Because of this, you know you have tremendous value
and worth in God's eyes. Because of the magnitude of
God's forgiveness and grace and his love for you, he is
worthy of your praise, gratitude, and love in return.

DIVINE PROMISE
HOW PRECIOUS ARE YOUR THOUGHTS ABOUT
ME, O GOD.   *Psalm 139:17*

Index

ABILITIES 1
ACCOMPLISHMENTS 2, 3
ACCOUNTABILITY 5
ADDICTION 7
ADVICE 9
AFFIRMATION 11
AGREEMENT 13
AMBITION 14
ANGER 15
APATHY 17
APOLOGY 18, 19
APPROVAL 21
ASSURANCE 22
BALANCE 24
BOREDOM 26
BROKENNESS 27, 28
BURNOUT 30
BUSINESS 32
BUSYNESS 33
CALL OF GOD 34
CHALLENGES 36
CHANGE 37, 39
CHARACTER 40, 42
CHURCH 43
COMMITMENT 45
COMMUNICATION 46, 48
COMPETITION 50
COMPROMISE 52
CONFESSION 53
CONFLICT 55, 56
CONSCIENCE 60
CONVICTIONS 61, 63
COURAGE 66
CRISIS 67
DANGER 69
DECISIONS 70
DEFEAT 71

DEPRESSION 73
DESIRES 75
DISCERNMENT 78
DISCIPLINE 79, 81
DISCONTENT 82
DISCOURAGEMENT 84
DOUBT 86
EMPTINESS 87
ENCOURAGEMENT 89
ENDURANCE 91
ENEMIES 93, 94
ETERNAL LIFE 96
EVIL 98, 99
EXAMPLE 101
EXCELLENCE 103
EXCUSES 104
EXPECTATIONS 106
FAILURE 107
FAITHFULNESS 109
FEAR 111, 113
FINISHING 114
FORGIVENESS 116
FUTURE 119
GENTLENESS 121
GENEROSITY 122
GOALS 124
GREATNESS 125
GRIEF 126
GUARDING YOUR
  HEART 128
HABITS 129
HAND OF GOD 131
HARD-HEARTEDNESS 132
HEART 134
HELP 136
HOLINESS 138
HOLY SPIRIT 139

Hope   140

Humility   142

Imagination   143

Impact   145

Impossible   146

Integrity   148

Intimacy   150

Investing   152

Joy   153

Kindness   155

Letting Go   158

Limitations   161, 162

Loneliness   164

Loss   165

Love   167, 169

Marriage   170

Meaning   174

Mercy   176

Mistakes   177

Motivation   181

Obedience   182

Opportunities   184

Opposition   186

Pain   188

Passion   190

Past   192

Patience   194

Peace   196

Perseverance   197

Perspective   199

Planning   200

Potential   202

Power   203

Power of God   204

Prayer   206, 208

Preparation   209

Presence of God   212

Pressure   214

Pretending   215

Pride   217

Priorities   218

Promises of God   220

Provision   224

Purpose   225

Quitting   227

Regrets   228

Relationships   231

Remembering   232

Renewal   234

Repentance   236

Reputation   237

Respect   239

Responsibility   240

Rest   242

Risk   244

Romance   245

Sacrifice   247

Seeking God   249

Self-Control   250

Self-Esteem   252

Serving Others   254

Sex   256

Sin   257

Spiritual Dryness   259

Spiritual Gifts   260

Spiritual Warfare   262

Strength   264

Stubbornness   266

Success   268

Surrender   269

Temptation   271, 272

Testing   274

Thankfulness   276, 278

Thoughts   279

Time   281

Tired   283

Tithing   285

Trust   287, 290

TRUTH *291, 293*

VALUES *294*

VICTORY *296*

VISION *298*

VULNERABILITY *300*

WAITING *301*

WARNINGS *303*

WILL OF GOD *304*

WISDOM *306*

WORDS *308*

WORK *310*

WORRY *312*

WORSHIP *313*

WORTH *315*

DIVINE
MOMENTS
Books

DIVINE
MOMENTS
for
WOMEN
*Everyday Inspiration
from God's Word*

DIVINE
MOMENTS
*Everyday Inspiration
from God's Word*

DIVINE
MOMENTS
for
MEN
*Everyday Inspiration
from God's Word*

DIVINE
MOMENTS
for
STUDENTS
*Everyday Inspiration
from God's Word*

DIVINE
MOMENTS
for
LEADERS
*Everyday Inspiration
from God's Word*